Special Needs, Special Plans

Navigating The Special Needs Financial Journey

Ashli Eaves, ChSNC®

Creative Ink Publishing

This publication is designed to provide accurate and authoritative information in regard to the subject matter covered. It is sold with the understanding that neither the author nor the publisher is engaged in rendering legal, investment, accounting, or other professional services.

This content is being provided for informational purposes only and should not be construed as specific recommendations or investment, tax, or legal advice. Consult with your investment professional before making important investment decisions. Always consult with the appropriate professional regarding your unique circumstances.

While the publisher and author have used their best efforts in preparing this book, they make no representations or warranties with respect to the accuracy or completeness of the contents of this book and specifically disclaim any implied warranties of merchantability or fitness for a particular purpose. No warranty may be created or extended by sales representatives or written sales materials. The advice and strategies contained herein may not be suitable for your situation. You should consult with a professional when appropriate. Neither the publisher nor the author shall be liable for any loss of profit or any other commercial damages, including but not limited to special, incidental, consequential, personal, or other damages.

Book Cover by Creative Ink Publishing

Illustrations by Ashli Eaves, ChSNC®

ISBN: 9798284186244

Contents

Preface IV

Introduction XI

1. The True Cost of Raising a Child with Special Needs 1

2. The Foundations of Special Needs Financial Planning 10

3. Government Benefits and Why You May Not Qualify 22

4. Special Needs Trusts 39

5. The Role of ABLE Accounts 55

6. Life Insurance 71

7. Expense Considerations for Education & Schooling 80

8. Other Tax Considerations & Write-Offs 101

9. Planning for Decision 113

10. Building a Strong Support Team 126

11. From Planning to Practice 142

Epilogue 149

12. What you should do now... 151

About the Author 154

Preface

WELCOME TO HOLLAND

BY EMILY PERL KINGSLEY

I am often asked to describe the experience of raising a child with a disability - to try to help people who have not shared that unique experience to understand it, to imagine how it would feel. It's like this......

When you're going to have a baby, it's like planning a fabulous vacation trip - to Italy. You buy a bunch of guide books and make your wonderful plans. The Coliseum. The Michelangelo David. The gondolas in Venice. You may learn some handy phrases in Italian. It's all very exciting.

After months of eager anticipation, the day finally arrives. You pack your bags and off you go. Several hours later, the plane lands. The flight attendant comes in and says, "Welcome to Holland."

"Holland?!?" you say. "What do you mean Holland?? I signed up for Italy! I'm supposed to be in Italy. All my life I've dreamed of going to Italy."
But there's been a change in the flight plan. They've landed in Holland and there you must stay.

The important thing is that they haven't taken you to a horrible, disgusting, filthy place, full of pestilence, famine and disease. It's just a different place.

So you must go out and buy new guide books. And you must learn a whole new language. And you will meet a whole new group of people you would never have met.

It's just a different place. It's slower-paced than Italy, less flashy than Italy. But after you've been there for a while and you catch your breath, you look around.... and you begin to notice that Holland has windmills....and Holland has tulips. Holland even has Rembrandts.

But everyone you know is busy coming and going from Italy... and they're all bragging about what a wonderful time they had there. And for the rest of your life, you will say "Yes, that's where I was supposed to go. That's what I had planned."

And the pain of that will never, ever, ever, ever go away... because the loss of that dream is a very very significant loss.

But... if you spend your life mourning the fact that you didn't get to Italy, you may never be free to enjoy the very special, the very lovely things ... about Holland.

When I first read *Welcome to Holland*, it stopped me in my tracks. Emily Perl Kingsley captured what so many of us feel but struggle to say—that shift from the life we expected to the life we've been given. Holland isn't where we planned to land, but it's where we are. And, like you, I've learned to see its quiet beauty, its different rhythms, and its unique challenges. That poem has shaped how I view not just parenting, but planning—because once you find yourself in Holland, the guidebooks need to change. That's where this book comes in.

When life hands you a map you never expected to navigate, you have two choices: get lost or learn to read the terrain. This book is about learning to read that terrain—specifically, the complex landscape of financial planning for families with special needs children.

For years, I viewed my life as a series of distinct lanes—separate paths that never seemed to touch. My career in education, my journey as a financial advisor, and my personal experience as a parent of a child with autism felt like parallel lines, each moving forward independently. But, over time, I've come to see these experiences differently. They're not separate lanes, but paths that have merged, creating a unique space of understanding and insight.

My journey began in a classroom, where I first discovered my passion for helping others. I learned the art of listening, of understanding individual needs. As an elementary school teacher, then a specialized educator in gifted programs, I thought I understood what it meant to support unique learners. Little did I know that my most profound lesson was waiting for me at home.

In 2012, our first son was born. Like many parents, we embarked on a journey of discovery—one that took us through a series of evaluations, screenings, and, ultimately, an autism diagnosis. This wasn't just a medical label; it was a new lens through which we would see the world. Much like putting on glasses for the first time, everything looked clearer, though not necessarily easier.

My career path eventually took a different turn. Feeling the pull of family and seeking new ways to make a difference, I transitioned from teaching to the world of financial planning. I became a financial advisor and, driven by a deep desire to understand and support families like my own, I eventually pursued the Chartered Special Needs Consultant (ChSNC) designation.

This book is born from that intersection—that magical place where my professional knowledge and personal experience overlap. It's for families who find themselves in uncharted territory, feeling overwhelmed by the financial complexities of raising a child with special needs. I don't claim to have all the answers, but I do have something valuable: a perspective shaped by walking this path myself.

My hope is to create a guidebook that feels less like a manual and more like a conversation with a friend who understands. A friend who knows that sometimes success looks different. That financial planning isn't just about numbers, but about creating opportunities, supporting growth, and creating more control over your financial direction to families navigating unique challenges.

We aren't just talking about numbers and investments. We're talking about creating possibilities. About understanding that financial planning for special needs families looks different—sometimes it means prioritizing therapy over vacations, investing in specialized education, or building a support network that goes beyond traditional arrangements.

To the families reading this: you are not alone. Your experiences are valid. Your challenges are real, and your love is extraordinary. This book is my way of reaching out, of saying, *"I see you. I understand. And together, we can find a way forward."*

Welcome to our shared journey. Welcome to Holland.

Special Needs, Special Plans emerged from countless conversations with parents who shared my worries. Over the years, I've sat across from hundreds of parents who, despite their education, resources, and determination, find themselves adrift in a sea of confusing legal jargon, contradictory advice, and mounting anxiety about their child's future.

This book was born from those conversations—from witnessing brilliant, capable parents reduced to tears by the complexity of creating financial stability while juggling careers and caring for their entire family.

The path to financial clarity shouldn't be this difficult, yet for families in the *"forgotten middle"*—those earning too much to qualify for many assistance programs but still feeling the weight of extraordinary care costs—the roadmap simply hasn't existed. Until now.

Beyond Traditional Financial Planning

The strategies that work for typical families often fall dangerously short for families with special needs children. A well-intentioned inheritance can disqualify your child from critical services. A robust college savings plan might be inappropriate when vocational training is the goal. Standard retirement calculations fail to account for potentially lifelong support requirements.

Traditional financial advisors rarely possess specialized knowledge in this niche, leaving families like yours to patch together advice from various sources, potentially with conflicting guidance. Mistakes in this arena aren't merely financial inconveniences—they can fundamentally alter your child's quality of life.

In these pages, I've addressed the topics and challenges that parents like you and I face. No abstract theories—just concrete steps, real-world examples, and actionable plans you can implement with confidence. **Intelligence and good intentions aren't enough in this specialized planning area**. You need a map designed specifically for the terrain you're navigating.

A Practical Path Forward

This book offers what I wish every family could have: clarity and confidence about their child's financial future, while trying to also navigate the present. I've organized the material to guide you from understanding basic legal structures to creating comprehensive financial strategies you can tailor to your child's specific needs.

You'll find step-by-step guidance on establishing special needs trusts, selecting appropriate trustees, calculating lifetime care costs, maximizing government benefits (even with higher income), and integrating planning for your child's future with your broader family financial goals.

Most importantly, you'll finish with a concrete action plan—not just concepts, but a timeline of what to do first, next, and beyond to help safeguard your child's future without sacrificing your family's overall financial health.

In Gratitude

I once heard someone say that we are a product of what others have poured into us and God's grace. As I reflect on the journey of writing this book, that sentiment rings truer than ever. This work is not just a collection of insights and strategies; it's the result of countless conversations, moments of encouragement, and the spiritual path that God has laid before me. I'm deeply grateful for the people who have shaped my thinking, shared their stories, and supported me through both personal and professional chapters of life.

First and foremost, I want to thank my husband. This journey hasn't been mine alone - it's been ours, every step of the way. Our partnership hasn't been just in marriage, but as teammates navigating the unique path of parenting and planning for our family's future. Your unwavering support, quiet strength, and ability to carry the weight with me, even when it's heavy, mean more than words can express. You've encouraged me when I doubted myself and stood beside me when the road was hard. This book may have my name on the cover, but your love and presence are woven into every page.

To my children, thank you for being my greatest teachers. Each of you, in your own way, has given me a deeper understanding of love, patience, and perspective. You continue to reshape how I view what's possible, and remind me daily of the beauty in simplicity and the strength of empathy. You are the reason this work matters so deeply to me.

This book exists thanks to the families who have trusted me with their most vulnerable hopes and fears. Their questions shaped my understanding, and their courage in facing difficult planning decisions has been profoundly inspiring.

To you, the reader: thank you for picking up this book. Your commitment to thoughtful planning reveals the depth of your love for your child. The road ahead may seem daunting, but you don't have to walk it alone. With the right tools and guidance, you can create a financial future that protects your child while honoring your entire family's needs.

The pages that follow offer a clear path through what often feels like an impenetrable financial and legal wilderness. My promise is that by the time you finish, the overwhelm you may feel today will be replaced with confidence, clarity, and a concrete plan for moving forward.

Let's begin the journey together.

Introduction

The Common Financial Concerns of Special Needs Families

If you're reading this, you're likely a parent or caregiver of a child with special needs. You love your child deeply, and you're doing everything in your power to provide the best life possible. Along with the joy and love they bring, they also create an enormous responsibility—one that goes far beyond what most parents experience.

You're not alone in feeling overwhelmed by the weight of financial decisions. Most special needs parents I work with share the same concerns:

- ***"I don't even know where to start."*** Between estate planning, trusts, government benefits, and long-term care, the sheer number of decisions can be paralyzing.

- ***"I worry about what happens when I'm gone."*** Many parents fear their child will be left without the financial support and caregiving structure they need.

- ***"We make too much to qualify for help, but not enough to feel financially secure."*** When you don't qualify for assistance but still struggle to cover the extra costs, it's easy to feel stuck.

- ***"I want to make sure all my kids are taken care of."*** Balancing financial planning for all your children—not just your special needs child—can feel like walking a tightrope.

- ***"My income doesn't feel like it goes as far as everyone else's."*** The additional costs of therapies, specialized care, and future planning can stretch finances thin, making it harder to build long-term security.

Sound familiar? If so, you're in the right place.

This book will to **simplify the process** so you can focus on what truly matters—**giving your child the best life possible without losing sleep over finances**

What You'll Gain from This Book

By the time you finish reading, you'll have a **concrete plan** to secure your child's financial future. You'll know:

- **How to create a financial strategy that works for your family's unique situation** (even if you don't qualify for government aid).

- **An understanding of different tools and legal options**—and how to decide what makes sense for your family from special needs trusts to guardianship decisions.

- **How to balance your child's needs with the rest of your family's financial future.**

- **What steps you should take now, in five years, and beyond.**

Most importantly, you'll walk away with **clarity, confidence, and guidance to help you make empowered decisions**, knowing you've done everything possible to protect your child's future.

This book isn't about throwing overwhelming amounts of financial jargon at you. It's about **giving you a clear action plan**—one you can actually follow.

Whether you read the entire book cover to cover or jump to the chapters most relevant to your situation, you'll walk away with practical, **immediately useful** knowledge.

This book is your map—your guide to helping you plan for your child's well-being not just today, but for the years to come. The key is **getting started**—taking one small step at a time.

Let's take that first step together.

Turn the page, and let's get started.

Chapter One

The True Cost of Raising a Child with Special Needs

The Diagnosis That Didn't Change the Needs

We went through test after test—hearing, vision, developmental screenings, even genetics. Each evaluation brought more questions than answers. We were chasing a diagnosis not because we needed a label, but because we thought it would unlock help. Insurance, schools, support programs—they all seemed to require a formal diagnosis before anything could begin.

When we finally pursued genetic testing, we thought, *"This will give us the clarity we need."* But the insurance company disagreed. They called it *"elective."* Denied. We were stunned. It didn't feel optional. We were trying to understand our child, to give him the best chance possible. And yet, we were told it wasn't necessary.

Diagnosis or not, we knew what we were seeing. Our child wasn't meeting milestones. He struggled with communication. Potty training felt impossible. We started piecing together what we could—physical therapy, speech therapy, Applied Behavior Analysis. Each service came with a cost, not just financially but emotionally, logistically. It felt like piecing together a life raft with whatever drifted by—just trying to stay afloat while the waves kept coming.

And even now, as he enters his teenage years, the costs haven't abated—they've just changed. We pay extra for Airbnbs so we can bring his dog who helps regulate his anxiety in unfamiliar places. We still seek therapy outside the school system to meet his unique needs. We know he'll likely live with us longer than most kids, which changes how we plan for housing and support. And it may sound small, but we've bought more pairs of glasses than I can count—because executive functioning challenges mean they're lost, stepped on, or forgotten almost as soon as they're replaced.

That experience taught me an important truth: you don't need a diagnosis to know your child needs support. And you can't wait for the system to catch up. You start where you are, with what you have, and build from there.

~Ashli
EAVES

When *"Making Good Money"* Still Isn't Enough

The misconception that higher income solves all financial challenges can be especially misleading for families of children with special needs. While many assume financial success creates a clear path forward, the truth is far more nuanced. For families earning above certain thresholds, doors to essential government programs and support systems often close, creating an unexpected paradox: those who appear financially secure on paper may actually face more complex planning requirements and fewer institutional safety nets.

For mothers who frequently bear the primary responsibility for both caregiving and financial management, the burden can be particularly heavy. Studies indicate that 69% of women are their households' primary decision-makers regarding financial investments. Furthermore, research suggests that women reinvest up to 90% of their income back into their families and communities. In households with special needs children, the demands intensify. A 2023 study revealed that 27% of caregivers spend 30 or more hours per week providing care, essentially committing to an unpaid part-time job. Career adjustments are also common; data shows that caregiving responsibilities have negatively affected the ability to save for financial goals for 64% of women in the "sandwich generation," who care for both children and aging parents. These compounded responsibilities make proactive financial planning not just important, but essential for caregivers and families managing the complex demands of both caregiving and long-term financial security.

The Planning Paradox

The financial planning required for a special needs child differs fundamentally from traditional planning approaches. While conventional wisdom suggests saving for college, retirement, and maybe a vacation home, parents of children with special needs must consider lifetime care that could span 50+ years beyond their own lives. This involves thoughtful and intentional planning strategies, legal structures like special needs trusts, and careful integration with existing financial commitments—all while navigating a complex web of regulations designed to protect government benefits that your family might not qualify for due to income thresholds.

Throughout this chapter, we'll explore three critical dimensions of this financial reality: the hidden costs that catch even the most prepared families by surprise; the complex relationship between income levels and assistance program eligibility; and effective strategies for balancing competing financial priorities across your entire family. By addressing these fundamental realities first, we establish the foundation for subsequent chapters covering legal protections, investment strategies, and long-term care planning.

My goal isn't merely to outline challenges, but to provide you with actionable frameworks that create clarity and confidence. The financial demands of raising a child with special needs present unique challenges, but, with proper planning and informed strategies, you can create a sustainable approach that helps protect your child while preserving your family's financial well-being. This journey begins with a clear-eyed assessment of the true costs involved—both financial and emotional—and continues with building a plan specifically designed for your family's circumstances.

As we progress through this book, we'll move from understanding costs to creating specific strategies that protect, plan, and provide for your child's future. Let's begin by examining what it truly costs to raise a child with special needs.

Beyond Medical Expenses: Hidden Costs You Haven't Considered

When parents first hear their child's diagnosis, their minds often race to doctor visits and medication costs. These medical expenses represent just the tip of the iceberg. The reality of raising a child with special needs includes a vast network of ongoing financial commitments that extend far beyond the doctor's office.

Think of these hidden costs like the underwater portion of an iceberg. While people focus on the visible peak—the medical bills that arrive in your mailbox—the larger mass lurks beneath the surface, silently straining family resources. These submerged costs include specialized therapies, adaptive equipment, home modifications, and educational interventions that insurance rarely covers in full, if at all. Even things like having to pay for lodging and meals for appointments that aren't available in your area, extra gas for additional travel, and additional fees for complex legal structures eventually take a toll on the budget.

According to research from Autism Speaks, raising a child with autism costs an average of $60,000 per year, with lifetime costs potentially exceeding $2.4 million. This can be compared to an estimated $176,000 to $407,000 for a child without disabilities. Other sources note that, on average, it costs about 17.8% more per year to care for a child with special needs. The stark reality is that these costs begin immediately upon diagnosis and often continue throughout your child's life. It's also further proof that your situation looks different. Therapies such as Applied Behavior Analysis (ABA) and occupational therapy, feeding therapy, and speech therapy aren't optional luxuries—they're essential interventions that help children develop necessary life skills.

Educational expenses create another significant burden. Public schools provide some services through Individualized Education Programs (IEPs), but parents may still choose to seek additional supports outside of the school setting to address areas that aren't directly tied to the learning environment. Private specialized schools can cost tens of thousands of dollars annually. Even families who choose public education may choose to supplement with private tutoring, educational consultants, and advocacy services.

Legal and administrative costs blindside many families. Creating a special needs trust with an experienced attorney can cost $2,000-5,000. Guardianship proceedings, necessary when a child turns 18 but cannot manage their own affairs, can run $3,000-10,000. Annual accounting and trustee fees add ongoing expenses. While every family's situation is unique, these legal tools are often essential components in planning for your child's long-term well-being.

The caregiving burden carries both direct and indirect costs. Specialized child care can cost 50-100% more than typical childcare. Many parents reduce work hours or leave careers entirely to manage their child's needs. This lost income—often hundreds of thousands of dollars over a lifetime—rarely appears in discussions about special needs parenting costs. A study by Autism Speaks found families lose an average of $18,000 annually in income due to increased caregiving responsibilities.

Transportation expenses multiply with frequent therapy and medical appointments. Families may need specialized vehicles with adaptive equipment costing more than the base vehicle price. Simple errands become complex logistical challenges requiring additional time and resources—a hidden cost rarely quantified in dollars but felt keenly in daily life.

Housing modifications represent another substantial investment. Widened doorways, ramps, accessible bathrooms, sensory adaptations, and specialized safety equipment can cost thousands of dollars. These modifications aren't covered by insurance, but are essential for safety and quality of life.

Many parents also face out-of-pocket costs for alternative treatments and therapies not covered by insurance. Special diets, supplements, sensory tools, and therapeutic equipment add thousands of dollars annually. Parents desperate to help their children try anything that might work, often without financial assistance.

For families in rural or underserved areas, the financial strain can feel even more intense—regardless of income level. Specialized services are often concentrated in major metropolitan areas, meaning families must travel long distances to access the care their child needs. In our case, we drove nearly three hours one way just to attend routine specialist appointments—sometimes more frequently when surgeries, evaluations, or additional therapies were needed. These added costs—fuel, time off work, lodging, and emotional energy—are rarely factored into traditional financial planning but can quickly add up.

Even families with insurance are surprised by hidden expenses. The Affordable Care Act improved insurance coverage for children with special needs by eliminating pre-existing condition exclusions and removing lifetime caps on benefits; however, private insurance may fall short of covering many essential services. Private plans may limit therapy sessions, exclude developmental services, or refuse to cover adaptive equipment or home modifications. Even families with excellent employer-provided insurance find that 30-50% of their special needs expenses remain uncovered.

The financial reality of raising a special needs child extends far beyond medical costs, creating a complex web of expenses that impact every aspect of family finances and require sophisticated planning strategies, especially if you are a higher income earner.

Balancing Your Family's Financial Priorities

Parents like us often find ourselves torn between competing financial priorities. The immediate needs of our children with disabilities can overshadow long-term planning for retirement, college for siblings, and overall family stability. Without careful balance, these competing demands create additional strain on already stressed family systems.

Many parents pour every available resource into their special needs child, hoping to maximize development and potential. This instinct, while understandable, can create long-term challenges for the entire family if not thought through. Retirement accounts remain unfunded, home maintenance gets deferred, and siblings' needs receive less attention and fewer resources. A sustainable financial plan should consider a balance between the immediate needs of your special needs child with the long-term security of the entire family.

Finding this balance resembles the airplane oxygen mask principle—secure your own mask before helping others. In a similar way, prioritizing your own long-term financial health can be an important part of planning for your child's future. If parents fully exhaust their retirement savings to cover current expenses, it may limit their ability to support their child down the road. Continuing to contribute to retirement, even while managing high out-of-pocket costs, can help protect the family's long-term stability and ensure that both parent and child have support over time.

Chapter Two

The Foundations of Special Needs Financial Planning

The Night I Knew We Needed a Plan

I'm a planner—Type A through and through. Oldest child. Stereotypical *"control enthusiast."* I love color-coded calendars, detailed checklists, and having backup plans for my backup plans. So in many ways, creating a financial and legal plan for our family felt like something I was made to do.

And yet—it didn't feel natural at all.

No matter how organized I was, I didn't know where to start. I wasn't even sure what questions to ask. I found myself comparing our situation to other families, wondering if we were doing enough, doing too much, or just doing it wrong. Some had already set up trusts. Others were talking about guardianship. Meanwhile, I was still trying to figure out what *"SSI"* even meant.

Then, one night, after the house was finally quiet, I read a story about a family who hadn't planned—and the chaos it caused after a parent unexpectedly passed away. No will. No trust. No roadmap for the future.

Their child had complex needs, and suddenly no one knew what to do. That story rattled me. That story rattled me. It made me realize that no amount of organization could substitute for real protection—and we didn't have it yet.

Another mom of a neurodivergent child once said to me, *"The best gift we can give our children is to make sure we've taken care of ourselves so they don't have to."* That stuck with me. Planning isn't just about the numbers or the paperwork—it's about peace of mind. It's knowing that even if life doesn't go according to plan, our family won't be left without one.

-Ashli

Start Where You Are

While most families plan around milestones like college and retirement, your roadmap includes lifelong care, ongoing medical or educational needs, and ensuring security well beyond your lifetime.

Think of it like planning a road trip: before choosing your route or destination, you need to know your starting point. That starting point—your current financial picture—becomes the foundation of every plan you build from here on out. Without it, even the most thoughtful plans can veer off course.

Many parents, understandably, operate in survival mode, constantly reacting to urgent needs like medical bills, therapy schedules, and navigating complex systems. But reactive planning—though often unavoidable—can lead to missed opportunities and long-term vulnerabilities. Shifting from reaction to intention begins with a clear understanding of where things stand today.

Know Your Starting Point: A Financial Planning Checklist

Before you can plan ahead, it helps to know where you're starting from. This isn't about perfection or having everything figured out—it's about understanding the pieces of your financial life today so you can make more informed decisions moving forward. Many families are surprised to learn they've already taken some great steps.

Take a moment to jot a few of these things down—or at least reflect on what you already know. You don't have to tackle it all in one sitting. Pick one area that feels manageable and build from there.

1. What You Earn & Spend

- List your sources of income, including wages and any government benefits.
- Track your monthly expenses—including both everyday costs and disability-related ones (like therapies or equipment).

2. What You Own & Owe

- Jot down your bank, investment, and retirement accounts.
- Include property, savings in your child's name, and outstanding debts like loans or credit cards.

3. How You're Protected

- Review your insurance coverage (health, life, disability).
- Check whether you have key legal documents in place—like a will, power of attorney, or special needs trust.
  Think about short-term caregiving plans and emergency savings.

Beyond the Typical Financial Roadmap

Most financial planning resources assume a fairly standard life path: education, career, retirement, inheritance. But for families with special needs, those steps may not apply—or may happen in a different order, on a different timeline, or not at all.

Your plan may also need to account for:

- Lifelong care and supervision for your child
- Maintaining eligibility for public benefits
- Legal protections for decision-making on behalf of your adult child
- Strategies to preserve assets without jeopardizing support

Specialized tools like special needs trusts, ABLE accounts, and structured insurance planning exist for exactly these situations—but they only work when coordinated with your overall financial picture.

Starting with a clear picture of your current situation provides a baseline for subsequent planning activities.

In the pages ahead, we'll walk through the unique considerations that come with financial planning for families like yours.

Why Your Financial Health Matters

It's natural to prioritize your child's needs first, but planning for your own financial well-being is not selfish—it's strategic. If your own retirement, long-term care, or insurance coverage is neglected, the long-term impact could fall on your child or other loved ones. A financially stable parent is one of the strongest supports a child with special needs can have. The truth is this: **your financial security is one of the greatest gifts you can give your child.**

The Balancing Act: Now, Later, and Legacy

Special needs financial planning isn't about choosing between your child's needs and your own—it's about finding the right balance between the present and the future. Examining your timelines and developing a coordinated plan can help you support your child while also preparing for your own financial well-being. Your planning must consider three overlapping priorities:

- **Now**: Daily care, therapy, education, and access to services
- **Later**: Planning for your own retirement, potential long-term care, and changes in income as you age
- **Legacy**: Putting a plan in place to help ensure your child is cared for after you're gone

This balancing act requires intentional trade-offs and coordinated planning—not one-size-fits-all advice.

Building a Parallel Plan: The Comprehensive Family Financial Framework

Just as you're planning intentionally for your child's needs, it's important to apply that same structure to your personal financial life. The two plans should work in tandem, not in competition. This structured approach helps families evaluate competing priorities while maintaining clarity. It consists of five interrelated categories:

1. Emergency Preparedness
2. Special Needs Care
3. Family Core Needs
4. Sibling Support
5. Future Security

These categories aren't static—they shift as your life evolves. Regularly reviewing and adjusting allocations helps ensure that no area is unintentionally neglected.

1. Emergency Preparedness

Every family needs financial stability to weather unexpected crises. For special needs families, this foundation becomes even more important to focus on maintaining:

- A liquid emergency fund covering 6-12 months of essential expenses
- Appropriate insurance protection (health, disability, life, property)
- Access to short-term credit for unexpected medical or therapy needs

Without this foundation, any financial disruption threatens the entire support structure for a child with special needs. Job loss, major illness, or home repairs could force devastating choices between basic needs and essential therapies.

2. Family Core Needs

This category covers essential expenses that benefit the entire family:

- Housing (mortgage/rent, utilities, maintenance)
- Basic transportation
- Nutritious food
- Basic clothing
- Primary healthcare for all family members

Core needs cannot be sacrificed without harming everyone, including your special needs child. The framework prioritizes maintaining stable housing and meeting basic family needs before funding additional therapies or interventions. A stable home environment provides the foundation upon which specialized care builds.

3. Special Needs Care

This category includes all expenses directly related to your child's special needs:

- Medical costs (doctor visits, medications, specialized treatments).
- Therapy services (speech, occupational, physical, behavioral)
- Educational supports (specialized schools, tutors, educational advocates)
- Adaptive equipment and assistive technology
- Home modifications and accessibility improvements
- Specialized childcare or attendant care

Parents should track these expenses separately from regular family expenses to more clearly monitor the true cost of special needs care. This tracking serves multiple purposes: documenting potential tax deductions, informing insurance appeals, and providing data for long-term planning.

4. Sibling Support

This category recognizes the importance of supporting all children in the family:

- Educational opportunities and college planning
- Extracurricular activities
- Respite care and family outings that benefit siblings

- Counseling or support services for siblings

Intentionally allocating funds to support siblings' development and well-being, preventing resentment and ensuring all children have opportunities to thrive.

5. Future Security

This category addresses long-term stability for both parents and the special needs child:

Many families sacrifice future security to fund current therapies, creating vulnerability as parents age. It's important to maintain at least minimal contributions to savings accounts, even during financially strained periods. Small, consistent contributions can compound significantly over time, helping to build long-term security.

- Understand and Maximize Employer Retirement Benefits

If available, employer-sponsored plans such as 401(k)s or 403(b)s can offer valuable opportunities for tax-deferred growth and retirement savings. If your employer offers a matching contribution, contributing enough to receive the full match can be an effective way to boost long-term savings.

- Automated Saving

Setting up automatic contributions—even at modest amounts—can make it easier to stay consistent over time. Depending on their goals, timeline, and comfort with risk, some families also explore different types of savings and investment options designed to grow steadily over time.

- Evaluate Your Insurance Coverage

  - Life insurance can help provide financial resources for your child's future or fund a special needs trust.

  - Disability insurance may help replace income if you become unable to work.

  - Long-term care insurance may help cover care needs later in life, preventing those costs from draining assets intended for your child.

- Create a Long-Term Care Plan—for Yourself

Many families focus primarily on planning for their child—but planning for your own care is just as important. This might involve exploring housing options, discussing future caregiving for yourself with loved ones, or modeling potential costs with a financial professional.

- Consider Alternatives Before Using Retirement Funds for Immediate Needs

Using retirement savings to fund current care needs may seem like a solution in the moment, but it can create challenges later. Early withdrawals often come with tax implications and can reduce your long-term financial security. Instead, families sometimes explore resources such as:

- Medicaid waivers and other public benefit programs (which we'll discuss in more detail later)

- Support from local nonprofits or grant-based assistance

- Special needs trusts funded through life insurance, which can help preserve other assets

Implementing this framework begins with thorough assessment of current spending across all categories. Many families discover significant imbalances—perhaps 80% of discretionary funds directed toward special needs care with minimal allocation to sibling needs or future security. Simply bringing these imbalances into awareness enables more intentional decision-making.

Monthly family budget meetings provide opportunities to realign resources according to changing circumstances. Using percentage-based allocation rather than fixed dollar amounts allows the framework to scale with income changes. For instance, a family might allocate 15% of after-tax income to future security, regardless of whether their monthly income is $5,000 or $15,000.

The framework doesn't prescribe specific percentages for each category—these vary based on family composition, the nature and severity of the disability, and available external resources. Instead, it provides a structure for making conscious choices about resource allocation rather than allowing urgent special needs expenses to automatically consume all available resources.

From Overwhelm to Action

Overwhelm is common. You're juggling care, advocacy, and daily responsibilities—adding financial planning can feel like too much. But you don't need to have it all figured out today.

Start with these small, manageable actions:

- Take stock of what you already have in place.
- Organize your financial and legal documents.
- Make a list of key professionals to contact.
- Identify your top three financial concerns.
- Use this list to guide your next conversation with a trusted advisor.

You don't need a perfect plan—you need a plan that evolves. This isn't about checking every box now. It's about laying one brick at a time and building a structure that supports your entire family, now and for years to come.

In the next chapter, we'll build upon these foundations by examining how to maximize government benefits while protecting your child's financial future. With each step, you're creating a thoughtful path forward that supports lasting well-being for your family.

Chapter Three

Government Benefits and Why You May Not Qualify

The System Said *"Denied"*

I thought our situation was clear. Our child had documented needs. He qualified for services at school. Therapists had written pages of notes detailing delays and support strategies. So when we first applied for government benefits—like Medicaid and SSI—I felt nervous, but hopeful. I thought we were doing the right thing. *"This will at least provide some relief,"* I thought.

We were told we *"qualified."* But that came with a catch: a spend-down—one that totaled thousands of dollars a month. Our case worker explained it like a deductible we'd have to meet before anything kicked in. But we weren't racking up thousands a month in medical bills (at least consistently), even with therapies and appointments. We had access to health insurance through employers. It felt like we technically qualified, but functionally we didn't. And that disconnect was infuriating.

At the time, I was a teacher. My husband had a comparable salary. Our household income wasn't even six figures, but apparently it was *"too much."* We applied for additional programs, like the one that covers health insurance premiums if you're over a certain income—but again, denied. Other options put us on years-long waitlists, or had eligibility rules that didn't seem to match reality.

We felt defeated. We were doing everything *"right,"* and still coming up short. It was a confusing web of regulations and requirements. No matter where we turned, we were stuck.

That was the moment I realized that **you can't just apply and hope**—you have to plan. Understanding how these programs work, how they don't work, and what they're actually designed to do became just as important as applying for them in the first place.

~Ashli

When The System Says *"No"*... Navigating the Benefits Maze

Many parents discover that the very government programs intended to support families like theirs can be frustratingly out of reach. It's a jarring realization—especially when you're already managing the daily demands of caregiving, therapy, and medical appointments. While it's common to approach government benefits as the primary financial solution, some families often run into unexpected barriers: income limits that are too restrictive, eligibility criteria that don't match their child's diagnosis, or benefits that simply don't meet their most urgent needs.

Programs like Supplemental Security Income (SSI) and Medicaid come with strict eligibility requirements, often reserved for families with the fewest financial resources. Many middle- and upper-middle-income households find themselves earning just above these thresholds, making them ineligible. But hitting these limitations isn't a dead end—it's a starting point for creating a more customized financial strategy. Even if benefits aren't currently accessible, they may play a role later, especially as your child approaches adulthood.

If your current financial situation doesn't qualify you for assistance today, don't assume that will always be the case. Circumstances change, programs evolve, and new options may become available down the road. Exploring these programs now helps you stay informed, prepared, and ready to act when the timing is right.

In this chapter, we'll break down the three most important elements of benefit planning. First, you'll get a clear overview of key programs like SSI and Medicaid, including how they work and who qualifies. Then, we'll look at how income and asset limits affect eligibility, using real-life examples to make these rules more understandable. Finally, we'll explore alternative financial strategies for families who may not qualify for benefits but still need long-term support solutions.

The goal isn't simply to qualify for the assistance immediately—it's to build a plan that truly supports your child, now and in the future. That might involve preserving access to public programs, or it may mean using private resources for greater flexibility. The best approach depends on your family's unique circumstances, priorities, and long-term vision. By the end of this chapter, you'll be better equipped to identify which strategies deserve your focus—whether they involve public benefits, private planning, or a thoughtful combination of both.

Understanding Important Life Stages for Your Child

When navigating this journey, specifically as we think about government benefits, it helps to think in terms of stages. Just like your child grows and changes over time, so do the services, supports, and eligibility rules tied to public programs. Understanding these transitions can help you prepare in advance to avoid gaps in care.

Early Childhood (Birth to Age 3)

This stage is all about early intervention. Programs like Part C of the Individuals with Disabilities Education Act (IDEA) provide services such as physical therapy, speech therapy, and developmental support—usually delivered in the home or childcare setting. These services are designed to catch delays early and lay a foundation for future success. Accessing these supports often starts with a developmental screening and evaluation, typically coordinated through your local early intervention agency or school district.

School Age (Ages 3 to 15)

Once your child turns 3, the responsibility for services shifts to the public school system. Under Part B of IDEA, your child may qualify for an **Individualized Education Program (IEP)**, which outlines the support and accommodations they need in the classroom. This stage focuses heavily on educational access and inclusion, but it also introduces services like occupational therapy, counseling, and behavioral support—provided through the school at no cost to the family.

High School Transition Years (Ages 16 to 21)

Around age 16, your child's IEP should start including a **transition plan**. This is a roadmap for moving from school-based services to adult life, including postsecondary education, vocational training, employment, and independent living. It's also the time to begin exploring Supplemental Security Income (SSI), vocational rehabilitation services, and other adult benefits. Planning early is key, as some services require waiting lists or proof of transition readiness.

Adulthood (Age 22 and Beyond)

After age 21 (or 22 in some states), public school services end and your child enters the adult support system. This often includes programs like Medicaid waivers, SSI, SSDI, housing assistance, and adult day programs. Eligibility is usually based on disability and income—not parental resources—making this a critical time to review financial and legal planning. The adult system can feel more fragmented than school-based supports, so early coordination is essential to maintain continuity of care.

By understanding these four key stages, families can be more proactive, plan ahead, and better advocate for their child at each turning point. Each stage brings new opportunities—and challenges—and planning for them helps you stay one step ahead on the journey.

Navigating the Benefits Landscape

Government benefits often serve as crucial lifelines for families caring for children with special needs. In the United States, several programs exist specifically to assist with the financial, medical, and developmental needs of children with disabilities.

Supplemental Security Income (SSI) is one of the primary federal programs, providing monthly cash payments to help meet basic needs like food, clothing, and shelter for children with qualifying disabilities whose families have limited income and resources.

Picture these benefits as a safety net—designed to catch those who might otherwise fall through the cracks of our healthcare and financial systems. Just as a safety net doesn't replace the ground beneath, these benefits don't solve every challenge, but they do provide essential support during difficult times.

Medicaid, another cornerstone program, offers comprehensive health coverage that often goes beyond what private insurance provides. For children with special needs, Medicaid can cover crucial services like physical therapy, occupational therapy, speech therapy, behavioral services, and durable medical equipment. Many states also offer Medicaid waiver programs that provide additional services to help children remain in their homes rather than institutional settings, even when family income exceeds traditional Medicaid limits.

Eligibility rules vary across programs, but most require both a financial and a medical determination. To qualify for programs like SSI and Medicaid, a child must meet specific definitions of disability. Generally, a child is considered disabled if:

1. **They have a medically determinable physical or mental impairment** (or combination of impairments),
2. **Which results in marked and severe functional limitations**, and
3. **The condition has lasted or is expected to last at least 12 continuous months** or result in death.

Additionally, there are strict income and resource limits that vary by state and family situation. Not every child with special needs will qualify—the determination hinges on both medical severity and financial circumstances.

Social Security Disability Insurance (SSDI) differs from SSI in that it's based on a parent's work history and Social Security contributions. Children with disabilities may receive SSDI benefits on a parent's record if the parent is deceased, disabled, or retired. Unlike SSI, SSDI doesn't have income and resource limits, but it does require that the disability began before age 22.

State-specific programs add another layer to this benefits landscape. Depending on where you live, your child might qualify for additional services like Children's Health Insurance Program (CHIP), state disability programs, or supplemental nutrition assistance. These programs often have different eligibility requirements and application processes than federal benefits.

The Affordable Care Act has also expanded protections for children with special needs, prohibiting insurance companies from denying coverage based on pre-existing conditions and removing lifetime caps on benefits—both critically important for children who may need extensive medical care throughout their lives.

Income Thresholds and Benefit Cliffs

Income limitations are one of the most challenging aspects of qualifying for government benefits like Supplemental Security Income (SSI) and Medicaid. These programs are intended to support families with significant financial and caregiving burdens—but the rules are often rigid, and many middle-income households find themselves earning too much to qualify, yet not enough to comfortably cover the cost of care.

Supplemental Security Income (SSI)

To determine SSI eligibility, the Social Security Administration uses a process called ***"deeming,"*** where both the child's income (if any) and a portion of the parents' income are counted. In 2025, the maximum federal SSI benefit for a child is $967 per month, but this amount decreases as countable family income increases.

The calculations are notoriously complex. They take into account **earned income** (such as wages), **unearned income** (like child support, interest, or other benefits), and the **household's composition**. For example, a two-parent, two-child household with one child with a disability will face different income limits than a single-parent household with two children. Even modest increases in parental income can significantly reduce or eliminate the benefit altogether.

To put this into perspective, a two-parent household with four members typically must earn less than about $75,000 annually to qualify for SSI benefits in 2025. That means a family earning $85,000—while still facing substantial disability-related expenses—could be entirely ineligible for assistance. This gap often leaves middle-income families feeling squeezed: earning too much for help, yet not enough to comfortably fund long-term care.

Medicaid and Medicaid Waivers

Medicaid is often the backbone of support for individuals with disabilities in the U.S., offering access to essential medical care, therapies, and in some cases, residential services. While the scope of coverage is broad, eligibility is often strict. In most states, a child's eligibility is based on household income. For a family of four, this typically means earning below $50,000 to $75,000 annually to qualify for traditional Medicaid or SSI-linked Medicaid.

However, eligibility varies significantly by state. In states that expanded Medicaid under the Affordable Care Act, families may qualify with incomes up to 138% of the Federal Poverty Level (FPL). In addition, many states offer Medicaid waiver programs that allow children with disabilities to qualify based on their medical needs, regardless of parental income. These programs can provide a vital path to services for families otherwise excluded by income thresholds.

The Benefit Cliff

Think of income limits like a series of steps leading down from a plateau. You might be standing comfortably on the flat surface of full benefits, but one small step forward in income could drop you to a lower level of support. Sometimes the step down is gradual; other times, it's a steep drop—a ***"benefit cliff"***—where exceeding the income threshold by even one dollar could result in the loss of thousands in benefits.

This creates a painful paradox: families may technically earn more, but end up with fewer total resources. Parents navigating this edge often face impossible choices—declining promotions, reducing work hours, or turning down raises—all in an effort to preserve essential benefits for their child.

Additional Eligibility Complexities

Resource limits add another layer to the equation. To maintain SSI and Medicaid eligibility, a child typically cannot have more than **$2,000 in countable assets**. This includes cash, savings, stocks, and property that could be converted to cash. Certain assets are excluded—such as the family home, one vehicle, and burial plots—but the $2,000 limit itself hasn't kept pace with inflation and continues to present challenges for families trying to plan responsibly.

Specific **income types** can also impact eligibility in unexpected ways. For instance, child support payments are considered **unearned income** to the child and can reduce SSI benefits nearly dollar-for-dollar after a small exclusion. On the other hand, certain **work incentives**—like the **Student Earned Income Exclusion**—allow children with disabilities to earn limited amounts without losing benefits, offering a small but important opportunity for independence.

Geographic Variability

Finally, geography plays a major role in benefit access. Because states administer Medicaid independently and often supplement SSI with their own payments, moving across state lines can dramatically change a family's benefit landscape. A benefit package that meets a child's needs in one state might be insufficient in another—creating invisible barriers to geographic mobility for families of children with special needs.

	Eligibility	Resource Limits	Health Coverage	Other Considerations
Medicare	Age 65+ OR younger with certain disabilities SSDI recipients after 24-month waiting period ALS patients qualify immediately	None	Part A (hospital insurance) Part B (medical insurance) Part D (prescription drugs	Funded by payroll taxes Premiums may apply for certain parts Not income or resource based
Medicaid	Low-income individuals SSI recipients in most states Children, pregnant women, elderly, and disabled individuals	$2,000 (individual) $3,000 (couple)	Covers hospital care, doctor visits, long-term care, and more	Jointly funded by federal and state governments Eligibility rules vary by state

	Eligibility	Resource Limits	Health Coverage	Other Considerations
SSI	Age 65+, blind, or disabled Limited income and resources	$2,000 (individual) $3,000 (couple)	Automatically qualifies for Medicaid in most states	Monthly maximum benefit ($967 individual, $1,450 couple) Funded by general tax revenues
SSDI	Disabled individual with sufficient work credits Work history of applicant of family member required	No resource limits	Medicare eligibility begins after 24 months of SSDI benefits; immediate for ALS patients	Monthly benefit depends on work history and earnings Higher benefits than SSI

Understanding the full spectrum of available government benefits requires persistence and attention to detail, as each program serves different needs and operates under unique eligibility rules based on disability severity, family income, and geographical location.

Scenario: Two Families, Similar Needs, Different Financial Realities

Imagine two neighboring families (see next page):

	Family A	Family B
Annual Income (pre-tax)	$55,000	$85,000
Child's Medical Costs	$50,000 (covered by Medicaid waiver)	$50,000 (paid out-of-pocket)
Tax Filing Status	Married Filing Jointly	Married Filing Jointly
Deduction Type	Standard Deduction	Itemized (medical expenses exceed standard deduction)
Deduction Amount	$29,200 (standard)	$43,625 (medical deduction)
Taxable Income	$25,800	$41,375
Estimated Federal Tax (2025)	$2,632	$4,501
Post-Tax, Post-Medical Cash Flow	**$52,368**	**$30,499**

While these numbers are simplified for illustration, they highlight how two families with similar care needs can experience very different financial outcomes. Despite earning more, Family B may have significantly less remaining for everyday expenses due to high out-of-pocket medical costs. Yet, under current program guidelines, they may not qualify for assistance. This scenario underscores how traditional poverty metrics don't always account for what some call *"medical poverty"*—when the cost of care dramatically reduces a family's financial flexibility, even with available tax deductions.

Even for families who meet the income and asset requirements for government assistance, support isn't always immediate. Long waitlists for services, especially Medicaid waiver programs, are a reality across much of the country. In parts of Mid-Missouri, for example, families may wait five years or more for certain services to begin. During that time, they're left to either pay out-of-pocket or go without critical therapies and supports. And for families with incomes above the eligibility threshold, getting on the list in the first place may not even be an option.

No matter where a family falls on this spectrum, understanding the interplay between government benefits and private resources remains essential. Every dollar saved, every trust established, and every benefit secured contributes to the same ultimate goal: ensuring the child with special needs receives appropriate care and maintains quality of life regardless of their parents' circumstances or longevity.

For families navigating this landscape, professional guidance often proves invaluable. Special needs financial planners, elder law attorneys, and disability advocates can help identify the most appropriate mix of government benefits and private resources for each family's unique situation. These professionals understand not just the technical aspects of benefits and planning tools, but also how they function in real-world scenarios for families of children with disabilities.

The intersection of care planning and financial planning cannot be overstated. The most meticulously designed financial plan will fall short if it doesn't align with the child's actual care needs and preferences. Similarly, the most compassionate care plan becomes unsustainable without adequate financial resources to support it. The two must develop in tandem, each informing and reinforcing the other.

Ultimately, the most successful special needs financial plans incorporate flexibility to adapt to changing circumstances. Government programs evolve, private resources fluctuate, and care needs shift over time. The ability to adjust strategies while maintaining core protections for the child with special needs distinguishes truly effective planning from rigid approaches that may falter when confronted with life's inevitable changes.

Whether through government benefits, private financial strategies, or—most commonly—a carefully calibrated combination of both, the goal remains constant: creating sustainable support systems that honor the dignity, preferences, and potential of each person with special needs while providing peace of mind to the families who love them.

Your Personalized Approach to Navigating the Benefits Landscape

Government benefits form a critical safety net for many families caring for children with special needs, but, as we've seen, not every family will qualify for these programs. The income limits and asset restrictions we've explored aren't simply bureaucratic hurdles—they represent important decision points in your financial planning process. For many higher-income families, these limitations often necessitate creative alternatives to ensure your child receives the care they need without sacrificing your family's financial security.

The strategies we'll explore aren't merely workarounds for benefit limitations—they represent a fundamentally different approach to special needs financial planning. Rather than adapting your family's financial life to government program requirements, we'll examine how to build a customized support system that addresses your child's specific needs directly. This might include specialized trusts, targeted insurance products, innovative investment vehicles, or strategic use of tax advantages designed specifically for families in your situation. The resulting plan will be as unique as your child, designed to grow and adapt as their needs—and your family's circumstances—evolve over time.

Remember that special needs planning isn't a one-size-fits-all proposition. Your child's specific diagnosis, prognosis, and needs will shape every financial decision you make. What works perfectly for another family might be completely unsuitable for yours. This is why the alternative strategies for higher-income families are valuable to explore—they offer customized solutions when standard government programs aren't accessible.

As you move forward, consider how the information in this chapter connects to your broader financial planning efforts. Whether you qualify for government benefits or need to create alternative funding structures, your next steps should include a thorough assessment of your child's long-term needs and your family's resources.

The private planning strategies we will discuss in this book will provide a pathway that doesn't depend on government eligibility. By combining insurance options, specialized trusts, and strategic investment vehicles, you can create a comprehensive safety net tailored to your family's specific situation.

Take time to review your current financial position against the criteria we've discussed. Are you near an eligibility threshold that might be worth restructuring your finances to meet? Or would your family be better served by focusing entirely on private funding mechanisms? These aren't simple questions, but answering them honestly is essential to developing a plan that will sustain your child throughout their life.

Your financial plan should reflect both your child's unique requirements and your family's distinct financial circumstances. By intentionally putting the principles in this chapter into practice, you're making a meaningful move toward building a secure future for your child—whether or not government benefits end up being part of the equation.

Chapter Four

Special Needs Trusts

What They Are and Why They Matter

The Heavy Weight of Love and Law

I remember the first time I heard the phrase *"special needs trust."* I was in a casual conversation with another parent after a therapy session. She mentioned something about setting one up for her son *"so his benefits wouldn't be affected."* I nodded politely, pretending to understand, but I had no idea what she was talking about.

Later that night, I started Googling. I read articles. I watched a few videos. And instead of feeling clearer, I felt overwhelmed. We have a basic will—did I mess something up? Was I supposed to have something else in place? Terms like grantor, trustee, and disbursements made it sound like something only wealthy families needed. I thought, "*Is this really something we should be doing right now? Is it too early—or already too late?*"

At the time, it all felt theoretical. But as our lives shifted and changed, so did our situation. With time, promotions, and career changes, our household income steadily increased. Now we're in a place where conversations about the future include the reality that we may leave a legacy to our children. What a blessing—but also, what a responsibility.

We still can't see the future. Our son shows us daily glimmers of independence and growth—but also reminders that he still needs more support than other kids his age. I don't know if he'll have a job one day that disqualifies him from certain government programs—or if those programs will be the backbone of his support as an adult. What I do know is that, as his parents, we feel a strong conviction to plan ahead and protect that eligibility in case it's ever needed.

So the question becomes: how do we create structures that allow us to leave something meaningful to both of our sons, in ways that fit who they are and what they'll need?

That's when I realized special needs trusts aren't about being wealthy—they're about being intentional. They're about putting protections in place so that whatever we leave behind actually supports our children without disrupting the benefits they may rely on. I know it feels frustrating—like an extra step that other families don't have to think about. But remember: our trip is different. Our view is different. And you're not the only one charting this course—others have walked this road. You don't have to navigate it alone.

~Ashli
EAVES

The Legal Document Every Special Needs Family Should Consider

Parents of children with special needs face an extraordinary set of financial and legal challenges that other families simply don't face on a regular basis. Between navigating government benefits, planning for lifetime care, and ensuring your child's quality of life, the task can feel overwhelming. At the center of this complex planning process stands one critical legal tool: the Special Needs Trust.

In this chapter, we'll explore the different types of Special Needs Trusts available to families and how each serves specific purposes. You'll learn the fundamental differences between first-party trusts, third-party trusts, and pooled trusts. **Understanding these distinctions is crucial** because they determine everything from who controls the assets to what happens to remaining funds after your child's lifetime.

We'll also address the practical question that keeps many parents up at night: *"How will we fund this trust?"* Many families mistakenly believe they need substantial wealth to establish a meaningful trust. The truth is that Special Needs Trusts can be funded through various means—including modest savings, life insurance policies specifically designated for this purpose, and thoughtful estate planning. You'll discover how to create a funding strategy that works for your family's financial situation, whether you're of modest means or more affluent.

Perhaps most valuable, we'll identify the common pitfalls that can undermine even the best-intentioned trust arrangements. From selecting inappropriate trustees to using overly restrictive language in the trust document, these mistakes can limit your child's options or even render the trust ineffective. **By learning from others' missteps, you can create a trust that truly serves your child's unique needs** while providing you peace of mind about their future care and quality of life.

The Special Needs Trust represents more than legal protection—it embodies your commitment to your child's lifelong security. When properly established and funded, it helps ensure that resources will be available to enhance your child's life beyond what government benefits provide, while preserving eligibility for those essential benefits. In the pages that follow, we'll transform this complex legal concept into a clear, actionable strategy that you can implement with confidence.

Understanding the Landscape of Special Needs Trusts

A Special Needs Trust isn't merely paperwork—it's a protective shield for your child's financial future. Without one, even well-intentioned financial gifts or inheritances can inadvertently disqualify your child from essential government benefits like Medicaid or Supplemental Security Income (SSI). These benefits often provide critical healthcare coverage and income support that would otherwise cost hundreds of thousands of dollars over your child's lifetime. As we talked about in the previous chapter, **the harsh reality is that just $2,000 in assets held directly in your child's name can eliminate their eligibility for these vital programs.**

Special Needs Trusts (SNTs) are specialized legal arrangements designed to help individuals with disabilities maintain their eligibility for government benefits while having access to additional resources. These trusts hold assets that supplement rather than replace public benefits like Supplemental Security Income (SSI) and Medicaid.

Think of a Special Needs Trust as a protective vault. Inside this vault, you can store assets that will benefit your child without those assets being counted against them when qualifying for government assistance. The walls of this vault are built with legal specifications that keep the contents secure while allowing controlled access for your child's needs.

There are three primary types of Special Needs Trusts: first-party trusts, third-party trusts, and pooled trusts. Each serves a specific purpose and follows different rules. Understanding these distinctions is crucial for making informed decisions about your child's financial future.

First-party trusts (also called self-settled trusts) are funded with assets that belong to the person with disabilities. These might come from personal injury settlements, an inheritance received directly, or accumulated savings. A key feature of first-party trusts is the payback provision. This means that when the beneficiary passes away, the state can recover costs for any Medicaid services provided to the beneficiary during their lifetime from the remaining trust assets.

The first-party trust works like a redirected river. The water (assets) that would normally flow directly to your child instead gets channeled into a carefully constructed reservoir (the trust). From there, the water can be released in measured amounts that quench their thirst for quality life experiences without flooding away their eligibility for crucial government support.

Third-party trusts are established and funded by someone other than the beneficiary. Parents, grandparents, or other relatives typically create these trusts using their own assets. Unlike first-party trusts, third-party trusts **don't** require a Medicaid payback provision. This means that after the beneficiary passes away, any remaining assets can go to other family members or designated beneficiaries according to the trust's terms.

Pooled trusts offer a simpler solution for families with limited resources. These trusts are established and managed by nonprofit organizations. Multiple beneficiaries' assets are pooled together for investment purposes, but each beneficiary has their own separate account. Pooled trusts can accept both first-party and third-party funds, though different rules apply to each. When first-party funds are used, Medicaid payback provisions typically apply.

The pooled trust operates similar to a community garden. Each family maintains their own plot, but shares resources, tools, and expertise with others. This creates economies of scale and provides access to professional management that might otherwise be unavailable to families with modest resources.

Each type of Special Needs Trust comes with its own set of advantages, limitations, and legal requirements. The right choice depends on your family's specific circumstances, the source of the funds, and your long-term goals for your child with special needs.

	First Party (a.k.a. Self-Funded)	Third Party	Pooled Trust
Funded By	Assets that belong to the individual with special needs (e.g. inheritance, lawsuit settlement)	Assets from parent, relative, or other third parties	Pooled assets from multiple individuals, managed by a nonprofit
Who Can Set It Up	Parent, grandparent, court, or competent individual; Beneficiary must be under 65 when established	Parent, grandparent, or court	Typically established by the individual or family with assistance from the nonprofit organization
Medicaid Payback	Yes	No	Yes
Trustee Options	Family member, professional trustee, or combination	Family member, professional trustee, or combination	Must use the nonprofit organization that manages the pooled trust

The S.H.I.E.L.D. Framework for Special Needs Trust Protection

In the intricate world of special needs financial planning, I find that families appreciate a clear, comprehensive approach. This acronym breaks down critical considerations for special needs trust protection, offering families a systematic method when considering their loved one's financial future.

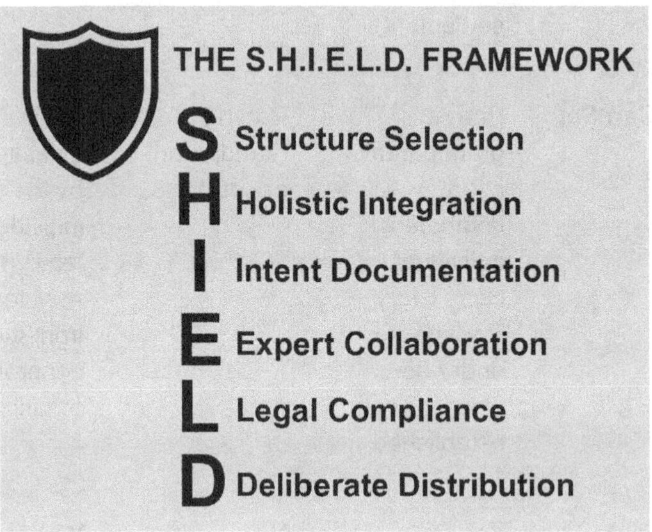

Structure Selection

The first component of the S.H.I.E.L.D. framework is choosing the right trust structure for your family's unique circumstances. This begins with understanding the key differences between **first-party**, **third-party**, and **pooled** special needs trusts. Each type serves a different purpose depending on the **source of the funds** and your **long-term planning goals**.

Selecting the appropriate structure isn't just a legal formality—it influences everything from **tax treatment** to how **remaining assets are handled after your child's lifetime**. Because of these lasting implications, this decision deserves thoughtful consideration in the context of your broader financial and family priorities.

Holistic Integration

The second component focuses on integrating the Special Needs Trust with your broader financial and estate plans. A trust doesn't exist in isolation—it must work in harmony with your will, life insurance, retirement accounts, and other assets to create a comprehensive safety net for your child.

Holistic integration means ensuring that all your financial arrangements direct assets to or around the trust as intended. This includes properly naming the trust as beneficiary when appropriate, ensuring your will contains the correct provisions, and coordinating with other family members who might wish to contribute to your child's future care.

Without this integration, you risk creating conflicts between different parts of your estate plan or leaving gaps that could compromise your child's financial security and benefit eligibility.

Intent Documentation

The third component involves clearly documenting your intentions for the trust and your wishes regarding your child's care. This goes beyond the legal requirements of the trust document to include guidance for future trustees and caregivers about your child's preferences, routines, medical needs, and quality of life considerations.

Intent documentation might take the form of a letter of intent, care guidelines, or supplemental trust instructions. These documents help future trustees understand not just what they can legally do with trust assets, but what they **should** do to best honor your vision for your child's life.

This documentation proves invaluable during trustee transitions or when decisions must be made about matters you couldn't have specifically anticipated when creating the trust.

Expert Collaboration

The fourth component emphasizes the importance of working with professionals who have experience with special needs planning. This includes attorneys who focus on special needs trusts, financial advisors who understand special needs planning, accountants familiar with special needs taxation, and benefit specialists who understand government program rules.

Expert collaboration helps ensure your trust is properly structured, adequately funded, and compliant with current laws and regulations. These professionals can also help you navigate the complex intersection of tax laws, benefit rules, and trust provisions that affect your planning.

Working with the right team not only helps avoid costly mistakes but also provides peace of mind that your plan incorporates best practices and current legal strategies.

Legal Compliance

The fifth component focuses on ensuring ongoing compliance with all applicable laws and regulations, including those governing public benefits like Medicaid and SSI. Benefit rules can be extremely complex and often change over time.

Legal compliance requires regular reviews of the trust document and its operation to ensure it continues to meet legal requirements and benefit eligibility rules. It also means staying informed about changes in laws that might affect your child's trust or benefits.

This component highlights the need for trustees who understand these complex requirements and the importance of ongoing professional guidance throughout the trust's existence.

Deliberate Distribution

The final component addresses how funds will be distributed from the trust to support your child. This includes defining clear guidelines for when it is appropriate to use trust assets, which types of expenses should be covered, and how those decisions should be made.

Thoughtfully crafted distribution guidelines protect against two common pitfalls: being too restrictive—limiting support in ways that hinder your child's quality of life—or being too permissive, which can lead to premature depletion of trust assets. These guidelines help trustees make consistent, well-informed choices that balance immediate needs with long-term financial security.

Importantly, these instructions should reflect your family's values and priorities, while allowing enough flexibility to adjust as your child's needs evolve over time.

The S.H.I.E.L.D. framework offers an integrated approach to Special Needs Trust planning, designed to safeguard your child's financial future and promote a fulfilling quality of life. Each component addresses a vital element of trust creation and administration, helping families sidestep common missteps and build a plan that truly works.

This begins with understanding the different types of Special Needs Trusts, followed by implementing thoughtful funding strategies and clearly defining how assets will be managed and distributed. When guided by a well-structured framework, these elements work together to preserve government benefits and provide the long-term support your child may need throughout their lifetime.

Funding Strategies for Your Child's Trust

Creating a Special Needs Trust is only half the equation. Equally important is developing a comprehensive strategy to fund the trust adequately. Without proper funding, even the most perfectly drafted trust document becomes merely a shell with limited benefit to your child.

Some families begin funding a third-party Special Needs Trust through regular savings. This approach allows you to build the trust's assets gradually, over time, while you're still alive. Dedicated savings accounts, investment portfolios, or even systematic monthly contributions can help grow the trust's value. Starting early, even with modest amounts, allows you to harness the power of compound growth over time.

Consider the various expenses needed throughout your child's lifetime. These could include supplemental medical care not covered by insurance, therapies, education, recreation, personal care attendants, and specialized equipment. The cost of these needs often far exceeds what government benefits provide. By analyzing these potential expenses, you can establish a clearer target for your funding goals.

Life insurance represents one of the most powerful tools for funding a Special Needs Trust. With relatively affordable premium payments, you can create a substantial death benefit that flows directly into your child's trust upon your passing. This approach provides what financial planners often call "pennies on the dollar" leverage—where a modest investment creates significant future financial security.

Several types of life insurance policies can work effectively for funding a Special Needs Trust. Term life insurance offers lower premiums and death benefit protection for a specified period. Permanent life insurance (including whole life, universal life, and variable life) provides lifetime coverage along with potential cash value accumulation. Second-to-die policies, which pay out only after both parents have passed away, often offer larger death benefits at lower premiums and align well with Special Needs Trust planning.

Estate planning represents another crucial funding mechanism. Your will can direct specific assets or a percentage of your estate to your child's Special Needs Trust. Similarly, you can name the trust as a beneficiary of retirement accounts like 401(k)s and IRAs, though this requires careful planning due to distribution rules. Real estate, investments, business interests, and other assets can all be directed to the trust through proper estate planning.

Other family members, such as grandparents, aunts, uncles, and even close friends, can contribute to your child's Special Needs Trust. This can happen during their lifetime through gifts or after their passing through their own estate plans. Sometimes, educating extended family about the importance of directing gifts to the trust rather than giving directly to your child can significantly increase the trust's resources while protecting government benefits.

When funding a Special Needs Trust, timing matters. Some families choose to fund the trust minimally during their lifetime, with provisions for substantial funding upon their death. Others prefer to fund the trust more robustly during their lifetime so they can oversee its management and ensure it's working as intended. Your approach should align with your overall financial situation, your comfort level with the trustees you've selected, and your child's current and anticipated needs.

The trust funding strategy isn't static—it should evolve as your family's circumstances change. Regular reviews with financial and legal professionals can help ensure your funding approach remains aligned with your goals, accounts for changes in the law, and adapts to your child's developing needs. As your financial situation improves, you might increase contributions. As trust laws or government benefit regulations change, you might adjust your strategy accordingly.

Common Pitfalls in Special Needs Trust Establishment

Setting up a Special Needs Trust requires careful attention to detail and a thorough understanding of both legal requirements and your child's unique needs. Despite their best intentions, families can unintentionally make mistakes that can compromise the effectiveness of the trust or even invalidate its benefits protection.

One of the most frequent errors is using generic, one-size-fits-all trust documents. Every child with special needs has unique circumstances, and the trust should reflect these individual requirements. Generic documents may miss crucial provisions that address your child's specific condition, needs, and life situation. They might also include language that inadvertently conflicts with eligibility requirements for government benefits.

Another common misstep is naming a trustee without fully considering the responsibilities involved. The trustee's role is demanding—requiring financial knowledge, understanding of government benefit rules, familiarity with the beneficiary's needs, and the time and willingness to fulfill ongoing responsibilities. Family members may seem like natural choices, but they might lack the necessary expertise or eventually face their own health or aging challenges. Conversely, professional trustees may have the expertise but lack personal knowledge of your child, while also requiring more in fees.

Failing to coordinate the Special Needs Trust with other estate planning documents creates another potential pitfall. If your will, life insurance policies, retirement accounts, or other assets don't align properly with your trust, you might inadvertently direct assets to your child outside the protective structure of the trust. This could trigger benefit disqualification or require expensive legal procedures to correct the situation after your passing.

The Vital Role of Special Needs Trusts

Setting up a Special Needs Trust represents one of the most crucial financial decisions you'll make for your child. As we've explored throughout this chapter, these trusts aren't just legal documents—they're protective shields for your child's financial future.

Remember that a Special Needs Trust is not a one-time decision, but part of an evolving strategy. As government regulations change, as your child's needs develop, and as your family's financial situation shifts, your trust may need adjustments. Working with professionals who specialize in special needs planning ensures your trust remains effective throughout your child's lifetime.

By establishing this critical financial tool, you're creating more than asset protection—you're providing a level of ***clarity*** in an uncertain future. Your child will have resources dedicated specifically to their needs while maintaining eligibility for essential government programs. This balanced approach offers both security and flexibility, allowing your child to thrive.

As we move forward in our financial planning journey, remember that the Special Needs Trust represents just one component—albeit a central one—of your comprehensive financial blueprint. In the next chapter, we'll look at how your Special Needs Trust interacts with other aspects of your planning to support overall coordination and continuity.

Chapter Five

The Role of ABLE Accounts

Not Now, But Not Forgotten

I remember when our son was first diagnosed, we got a call a few weeks later from a social worker. She was kind, energetic, and eager to help—but the conversation felt like drinking from a firehose. There were what felt like a million things to do and dozens of resources to explore.

One of the things she mentioned was an ABLE account. I can still hear her voice—excited and upbeat—telling me how new and groundbreaking it was, how important it would be for our son's future. She raved about it as if it were the answer to everything. And maybe, in some ways, it could have been a great tool to use. But at the time, I was drowning in emotion, paperwork, and grief for the expectations I didn't even know I'd been carrying.

To be honest, I didn't dig much into it. I was treading water in other ways—processing new medical terms, adjusting our routines, fielding questions from family, and trying to keep up with what each day brought. It didn't didn't rise to the same level of importance of things I needed to learn about right now.

It wasn't until a few years later—after a career pivot into the financial world—that I circled back to ABLE accounts. This time, I saw them through a completely different lens. The tax advantages, the flexibility, and the way they could be used to supplement benefits without jeopardizing eligibility—it all clicked. This wasn't just another account. It was a way to give our son dignity, options, and independence down the road.

Now, we use a combination of 529 and ABLE accounts. The 529 helps us address tuition today. The ABLE account offers a tool for future expenses—giving us breathing room to support him in the way he'll need, when he needs it.

And the irony? It's probably one of the easiest financial steps we've taken—yet it's still one that many families don't know about. It sat on the back burner for us for years. Now I see it for what it is: a simple but powerful way to plan ahead, without adding more to your plate—and with the potential to make a meaningful difference when it matters most.

~Ashli EAVES

Beyond Savings: How ABLE Accounts Can Change Your Family's Financial Future

Creating financial security for a child with special needs requires more than standard savings accounts and traditional estate planning. The 2014 introduction of ABLE (Achieving a Better Life Experience) accounts fundamentally changed the landscape of special needs financial planning, offering families a powerful tool that complements established strategies like Special Needs Trusts.

Understanding ABLE accounts isn't just helpful—it's becoming essential. These accounts have opened up new possibilities, allowing individuals with disabilities to save meaningful amounts of money without putting vital government benefits like Supplemental Security Income (SSI) and Medicaid at risk. For many families, this addresses a long-standing and deeply personal challenge: how to support a loved one financially without jeopardizing access to the programs they depend on for daily care and long-term stability.

Incorporating ABLE accounts into a broader estate plan can significantly strengthen your child's financial future. While special needs trusts remain a foundational tool in long-term planning, ABLE accounts bring a level of flexibility and everyday accessibility that trusts alone often can't provide. **When used together, these planning tools complement one another—preserving benefits eligibility while expanding the resources available to support your child's quality of life now and in the years to come.**

Many parents mistakenly view ABLE accounts and Special Needs Trusts as interchangeable, but each serves a unique role within a well-rounded financial strategy. This chapter will clarify those differences, helping you determine when and how to use each tool effectively. We'll also explore one of the most common challenges families face—timing. Knowing when to establish these accounts and how to fund them thoughtfully requires careful consideration of your child's current needs, long-term goals, and overall financial picture. You'll find practical guidance on when to open an

ABLE account, smart funding strategies, and how to integrate this flexible tool into your broader financial and estate planning.

By understanding the specific roles, limitations, and advantages of ABLE accounts within your overall plan, you'll be better equipped to make informed decisions that protect your child's future. The integration of these accounts with traditional estate planning tools—like Special Needs Trusts, wills, powers of attorney, and life insurance—creates a comprehensive strategy that addresses both immediate needs and long-term security. This holistic approach is designed to help your child access the resources they may need throughout their lifetime, regardless of what the future may hold.

Understanding ABLE Accounts: A Financial Tool for Special Needs

ABLE accounts provide a unique opportunity for individuals with disabilities to save money without impacting their eligibility for government benefits. These tax-advantaged savings accounts, established through the Achieving a Better Life Experience (ABLE) Act of 2014, allow qualified individuals to set aside funds for disability-related expenses while maintaining access to programs like Supplemental Security Income (SSI) and Medicaid.

Since this program is not needs based, there is no income threshold for families that want to establish this account. Think of an ABLE account as a specialized savings jar that remains invisible to benefit assessors up to certain limits. Most government assistance programs limit recipients to $2,000 in countable assets. Without ABLE accounts, families faced a painful choice: remain in poverty to keep benefits or lose critical support by saving for future needs. This created a financial trap that was nearly impossible to escape.

ABLE accounts are a flexible, tax-advantaged savings tool designed specifically for individuals with disabilities. To qualify, the individual's disability must have begun before age 26—but starting January 1, 2026, the ABLE Age Adjustment Act will raise that threshold to age 46, expanding eligibility for many more families. Each beneficiary can have only one ABLE account, and contributions—up to $19,000 annually as of 2025—grow tax-free when used for qualified disability expenses. These can include housing, education, transportation, healthcare, assistive technology, personal support services, and even basic living costs—essentially, anything that helps maintain or improve quality of life. Importantly, the first $100,000 in an ABLE account is excluded from SSI asset limits, helping families save without risking eligibility for government benefits. For example, a $10,000 contribution that grows 15% over time would yield $1,500 in tax-free earnings when used appropriately. Each state sets a lifetime contribution cap, but the ability to grow and access funds tax-free—while preserving benefits—makes ABLE accounts a powerful planning option.

Grandparents, extended family, and friends can contribute to an ABLE account, helping to build a broader network of financial support. These gifts are not considered income to the beneficiary, which means they can be made without affecting eligibility for government benefits. Contributions are often made for birthdays, holidays, or other milestones, turning special occasions into opportunities to support long-term needs. It's important to note that total contributions from all sources cannot exceed the annual limit. For example, in 2025, if parents contribute $12,000, other friends or family members could collectively contribute up to $7,000 more to stay within the $19,000 limit. Funds from a 529 college savings plan can be rolled over into an ABLE account, but it's important to note that the rollover amount also counts towards the annual contribution limit.

A notable exception to this rule occurs when the designated beneficiary (individual with special needs) is employed and generating taxable income. Under these circumstances, the individual may supplement their ABLE account contributions beyond the annual limit. The additional contribution is capped at the lesser of two values: the beneficiary's total compensation that qualifies as gross income for the tax year, or the Federal Poverty Level for a single-person household, which is $15,060 in 2025.

Setting up an ABLE account is relatively simple compared to other financial planning tools. Most states offer ABLE programs, and you can often enroll in any state's program regardless of where you live. This allows families to shop for features that best suit their needs—lower fees, better investment options, or specific program benefits. Many programs offer enrollment online with minimal paperwork and low minimum deposits. While there is no federal tax deduction for these accounts, some states do offer a state deduction, so be sure to look into the specifics where you live.

The impact of ABLE accounts extends beyond mere dollars and cents. For many families, these accounts represent the first opportunity to save for their loved one's future. Parents can experience emotional relief when finally being able to put aside funds for their child's future needs without worrying about benefit eligibility reviews or program disqualification. It also gives parents peace of mind knowing they're saving in a way that aligns with their child's unique circumstances—especially when compared to traditional 529 plans (usually thought of as "college savings" plans), which come with stricter rules about how the money can be used. For families focused on flexibility and comprehensive support, ABLE accounts often feel like a more practical, compassionate choice.

As you consider how ABLE accounts can fit into your overall plan, it's worth highlighting one especially empowering feature: these accounts can be managed directly by the individual with disabilities when appropriate, promoting independence, financial literacy and confidence. For those who need assistance, parents, guardians, or authorized representatives can step in to manage the account. This flexibility allows the arrangement to adapt over time, growing alongside the individual's needs, skills, and circumstances.

ABLE accounts create a critical financial bridge between government benefits and personal savings, allowing families to plan for their child's future without sacrificing essential support today.

ABLE Accounts vs. Special Needs Trusts

ABLE accounts and Special Needs Trusts (SNTs) serve similar purposes—protecting assets while maintaining benefit eligibility—but they function quite differently. Understanding these differences is crucial for creating an effective financial strategy for your child with special needs.

Special Needs Trusts are legal arrangements managed by trustees. These structured entities can hold unlimited assets and can be funded with virtually any type of property—real estate, investments, life insurance proceeds, or personal property. Unlike ABLE accounts, there are no annual contribution limits for SNTs. A trust can receive millions of dollars from an inheritance or settlement without jeopardizing benefits. This makes SNTs essential for larger sums of money or when planning for lifetime care needs.

Control structures differ significantly between these two tools. ABLE accounts can be managed by the beneficiary if they have capacity, promoting independence, choice and control. In contrast, SNTs require trustees who make all disbursement decisions according to the trust document and relevant laws. This oversight provides protection but reduces autonomy for the beneficiary.

The age requirement presents another critical distinction. ABLE accounts are only available to those whose disability onset occurred before age 26 (soon to be age 46 starting in January 2026). This restriction excludes many people with disabilities acquired later in life. In contrast, Special Needs Trusts have no such age limitations and can be established for anyone who meets the disability criteria regardless of when the disability began.

Distribution rules create another significant difference. ABLE account funds must be used for *"qualified disability expenses,"* which—while broadly defined—do create limitations. SNTs have more flexibility in how funds can be used, though distributions must still supplement rather than replace government benefits. Additionally, ABLE accounts can pay for housing expenses without affecting SSI benefits, while SNT payments for housing can reduce SSI payments.

Medicaid recovery represents a crucial consideration. After the death of an ABLE account beneficiary, remaining funds may be subject to Medicaid payback claims for services provided during the account's existence. Third-party Special Needs Trusts (those funded by parents or others) have no such payback requirement, allowing remaining assets to pass to other family members. This distinction makes SNTs preferable for inheritance planning.

Setup complexity and costs differ substantially. An ABLE account can be established online in minutes with minimal expense—often just a small enrollment fee and annual maintenance charges of $30-$60. Special Needs Trusts typically require an attorney's assistance, costing $2,000-$5,000 for proper drafting, plus ongoing trustee fees if professional management is needed.

Tax treatment varies between these options as well. ABLE accounts grow tax-free when used for qualified expenses, similar to 529 college savings plans. Trusts face compressed tax brackets, potentially resulting in higher tax rates on investment growth. This tax advantage makes ABLE accounts more efficient for accumulating modest savings over time.

The ownership structure creates additional distinctions. ABLE accounts belong to the beneficiary, who may have control over the funds depending on their capacity. SNTs create a more protective arrangement where the beneficiary has beneficial interest but no direct control. This distinction becomes important when considering the beneficiary's ability to manage finances responsibly.

How might combining both ABLE accounts and Special Needs Trusts in your financial planning create a more comprehensive safety net that maximizes benefits while providing both short-term flexibility and long-term security?

ABLE Account	Special Needs Trust (SNT)
Helps cover day-to-day expenses for individuals with disabilities without affecting eligibility for government benefits.	Protects larger sums of money (like inheritances or legal settlements) while preserving benefits eligibility.
Individual with a qualifying disability, family member, or legal guardian.	Typically established by parents, guardians, or a court-appointed trustee; can be set up by the beneficiary if it's a first-party trust. Address medical debt, explore support resources.
Individual must have a qualifying disability with onset before age 26 (age 46 beginning in 2026).	No age restriction for third-party trusts; first-party trusts require the beneficiary to be under age 65 when funded. More for medical or benefit disruptions.
$19,000 per year (2025 limit; subject to change annually).	No annual contribution limit, but gifts over the federal exclusion may trigger tax reporting.
The beneficiary can potentially manage the account, depending on capacity and age.	Managed by a trustee who controls how and when funds are used. Leverage medical expense deduction, play around trust tax rules.
Must be used for qualified disability expenses (broadly defined).	Can be used for nearly any purpose that benefits the individual with special needs (except food and shelter in some cases, depending on trust type).
Balances under $100,000 do not affect SSI; Medicaid is not impacted regardless of balance.	Properly structured trusts do not affect SSI or Medicaid eligibility.
Upon the beneficiary's death, any remaining funds may be claimed by Medicaid.	First-party trusts require Medicaid payback; third-party trusts do not.
Generally low or no setup cost; may have small annual fees.	Can be costly to establish (legal fees) and maintain (trustee and administration fees).

Investment Considerations for Both Tools

Investing decisions differ significantly between ABLE accounts and Special Needs Trusts. These differences reflect their distinct purposes and time horizons within your overall financial strategy.

ABLE accounts typically offer investment options similar to 529 college savings plans—a selection of mutual funds or pre-designed portfolios with varying risk levels. Most programs provide choices ranging from conservative (mostly cash and bonds) to aggressive (primarily stocks). Your selection should align with when your child will need the funds. Money needed within a few years should remain in conservative options, while funds for expenses many years away might benefit from growth-oriented investments. Because the right strategy depends on your unique timeline and risk tolerance, this is a great time to consult a financial advisor who understands special needs planning and can help tailor the investment approach to your family's goals.

Special Needs Trusts can hold virtually any type of investment, from basic bank accounts and mutual funds to real estate and privately held businesses. This flexibility allows for sophisticated investment strategies tailored to the beneficiary's long-term needs. Professional trustees often work with financial advisors to create diversified portfolios designed for long-term growth and income generation.

Risk management looks different for each tool as well. ABLE accounts benefit from the relative simplicity of preset investment options, but this simplicity also limits customization. Trusts offer greater customization but require more active management and oversight. This distinction highlights why professional financial advice is particularly valuable when managing trust investments.

The taxation differences between these accounts can also affect how the funds are invested. Since ABLE accounts grow tax-free when used for qualified expenses, they're often better suited for investments that might otherwise create taxable income. In contrast, Special Needs Trusts are subject to higher tax rates on income at lower thresholds, so it's important to consider more tax-efficient strategies—such as using investments that generate less taxable income or exploring options like tax-exempt municipal bonds.

Strategic Planning Across a Lifetime: Using ABLE Accounts and Special Needs Trusts Together

Effective financial planning for a child with special needs involves more than just choosing the right tools—it requires a thoughtful strategy that evolves over time. Both ABLE accounts and Special Needs Trusts (SNTs) serve important but distinct roles, and, when used together, they can provide a flexible, secure framework that can support throughout your child's life.

Timing and Implementation Matter

ABLE accounts are most effective when opened early, even with modest initial funding. Doing so allows for more potential tax-free growth and gets the infrastructure in place for future contributions. Families often begin funding ABLE accounts with birthday or holiday gifts, or even a child's own earned income from part-time work. Because ABLE contributions are not considered income to the beneficiary and the first $100,000 in the account is excluded from SSI asset limits, these accounts provide a valuable way to save without impacting eligibility for benefits.

Special Needs Trusts, by contrast, are generally used as long-term planning vehicles and are often funded through estate plans or life insurance proceeds. Parents typically designate the trust as the beneficiary of assets such as retirement accounts, insurance policies, or other financial resources to be transferred after their death. These trusts can also be funded during a parent's lifetime but are more commonly structured to receive assets later on. SNTs are designed to hold larger sums while protecting benefit eligibility, and they can be used to pay for housing support, medical treatments not covered by Medicaid, personal care attendants, and other quality-of-life expenses.

Using Both Tools Strategically

In practice, many families find it helpful to use ABLE accounts for current and near-term supplemental needs—such as therapy not covered by insurance, assistive technology, or transportation—while reserving the trust for larger, long-term expenses. One advantage of using both tools together is that a trustee can make distributions from the SNT into the ABLE account (within the annual contribution limit), making it easier to access funds for day-to-day expenses while still preserving the protections of the trust.

This strategy can evolve throughout the beneficiary's life. During childhood, an ABLE account might be used for extracurricular activities, sensory equipment, or specialized therapies. In young adulthood, it could fund job training, commuting expenses, or a laptop for college. Later in life, the SNT can step in to provide for supplemental housing, in-home care, or enrichment opportunities that enhance independence and quality of life.

Customizing to Fit Your Family's Needs

It's important to evaluate your family's specific situation when deciding how to use each tool. If your child developed a disability after the current ABLE age threshold, they won't be eligible for an account, making the trust your primary option. Conversely, if assets are relatively modest and your child is capable of managing some of their own finances, an ABLE account may offer enough flexibility without the added complexity of trust administration.

Keep in mind that ABLE accounts are relatively easy to manage, often functioning like a checking or savings account with investment options and minimal reporting requirements. Special Needs Trusts, however, require more oversight: a designated trustee, careful record-keeping, and separate tax filings. For that reason, many families limit the trust's use to larger, infrequent expenses or long-term reserves.

Long-Term Considerations and Evolving Needs

Lifetime planning should also consider the impact of changing laws and benefit programs. Government systems are not static, and what works today may change in the future. Maintaining both an ABLE account and a Special Needs Trust provides the flexibility to adapt if eligibility requirements or program benefits shift over time.

Involving extended family members in your strategy is also critical. Well-intentioned relatives may inadvertently leave assets directly to your child, which could disqualify them from benefits. A simple one-page explainer can go a long way in helping others understand how to support your child—whether by contributing to an ABLE account or designating the SNT as a beneficiary.

By thinking ahead and implementing these tools strategically, you can create a coordinated plan that supports your child now, prepares for the future, and protects access to essential services and resources. The combination of an ABLE account's flexibility and a Special Needs Trust's long-term security offers a strong foundation for lifetime planning.

Getting Started with an ABLE Account: A Simplified Action Plan

Step 1: Confirm Eligibility

Make sure your child meets the ABLE account requirements—specifically, that the disability began before age 26 (expanding to 46 in 2026). Gather basic documentation like a disability diagnosis and identification.

Step 2: Compare State Programs

You're not limited to your home state—look at a few ABLE programs to compare fees, investment options, and online tools. Some states even offer tax incentives for residents, so it's worth checking.

Step 3: Open the Account

Once you've chosen a program, head to their website and complete the online application. You'll need your child's personal details and banking information to set up contributions.

Step 4: Fund and Track

Decide whether you'll contribute a lump sum or make regular deposits. Keep track of your contributions so you don't exceed the annual limit. It's also helpful to start a simple system for tracking withdrawals and saving receipts for qualified disability expenses.

Step 5: Coordinate with Your Broader Plan

Talk with your financial advisor to ensure your ABLE account works alongside your Special Needs Trust or other long-term planning tools. The goal is to make sure each piece of your plan complements the others.

Step 6: Review Regularly

Check in on your ABLE account every few months to review performance, contributions, and expenses. Stay informed about any legislative updates that could affect how you use the account.

The financial decisions you make today create ripple effects throughout your child's future. By understanding how ABLE accounts function within your broader financial landscape, you're taking concrete steps toward creating stability and independence. This knowledge transforms uncertainty into action, giving you confidence that you're building a financial framework that will support your child for a lifetime.

Remember that financial planning for special needs is not static. As regulations change and your child's needs develop, regularly revisit your strategy with qualified professionals who specialize in special needs planning. This proactive approach ensures that the financial foundation you're building remains solid for years to come.

Chapter Six

Life Insurance

Planning Ahead in an Uncertain World

The Thing I Didn't Want to Think About

Life insurance was one of those topics I kept avoiding. Not because I didn't think it was important—I knew it was. But because even saying the words out loud felt heavy. Like tempting fate. Like admitting that one day I really won't be here.

For a long time, I told myself we had time. That I'd get to it *"soon."* I'd justify not having it because we *"didn't have the budget"*. But the truth is, I just didn't want to face it. When you have a child with disabilities, there's a unique kind of fear that creeps in during quiet moments. What if I'm not here to help him? Who will understand his needs like I do? Who will advocate for him? And will there be enough—money, support, structure—to sustain him when I'm no longer here to provide?

Eventually, those questions became louder than my avoidance. I realized that not planning was its own kind of decision—one that left too much to chance.

My first experience in the financial world—after stepping away from teaching—was selling life insurance. Through many conversations with clients, it became clear that it's not the glamorous, *"fun"* part of planning. But it was the piece that made everything else work. It's what gives families time to figure things out. It's what can provide grieving parents room to breathe. And it's when I realized... this is the part no one wants to talk about, but everyone needs.

I also came to understand something else: life insurance isn't just about leaving something behind. It's about protecting what we're building right now. If something were to happen to me or my husband during these years—while we're raising our boys, juggling therapies, managing school meetings, and covering the cost of everyday life—it would be more than emotionally devastating. It could be financially destabilizing.

Life insurance is our way to protect each other, not just our kids. A way to soften the financial blow in the midst of grief. A way to make sure there's space to grieve, to adjust, to keep going without the added weight of financial chaos.

Today, we think of it as a building block in our overall plan. A way to replace lost income. A gift that says, *"You're still protected. Even if I'm not there."*

It's not easy to think about. But once it was in place, it brought a kind of peace I didn't expect because now we've done what we can to prepare for even the hardest *"what ifs."*

Why Life Insurance Matters for Special Needs Families

For families navigating the complexities of raising a child with special needs, planning for the future isn't just about saving for college or ensuring a comfortable retirement—it's about creating a lasting financial structure that provides support long after you're gone. Among all the financial tools available, life insurance stands out as a uniquely powerful instrument in building that legacy of care.

Unlike investments or savings accounts that accumulate slowly over time, life insurance provides something few other financial tools can: immediate, tax-free protection at the moment it's needed most. For any family, it offers a safety net to help replace lost income, settle debts, or provide for loved ones. But for families supporting a child with special needs, it plays an even more critical role. It can help ensure that care, advocacy, and financial resources continue–long after parents are gone. That's why life insurance is not just a helpful tool: it's a foundational element in long-term financial planning.

In any financial plan, the goal of life insurance is to replace lost income or provide for dependents. But for parents of children with disabilities, the stakes are even higher. Your child may never be financially independent, and the costs associated to maintain care—medical needs, therapies, housing, transportation, and more—can continue throughout their lifetime.

A well-structured life insurance policy can:

- **Fund a special needs trust**, preserving eligibility for government benefits like Medicaid and SSI.

- **Provide for long-term care and living expenses** that go beyond what public programs cover.
- **Offer peace of mind,** knowing your child will have a stable financial foundation even after your passing.
- **Equalize your estate**, ensuring all your children are provided for in ways that reflect their individual needs.

Types of Life Insurance to Consider

Understanding your options is the first step. There are four main types of life insurance that may play a role in your plan:

1. **Term Life Insurance**: Offers affordable coverage for a set period (e.g., 10, 20, or 30 years). Best used for temporary needs, such as covering income while children are young or paying off debt.

2. **Whole Life Insurance**: Provides lifelong coverage with fixed premiums and a guaranteed cash value that grows over time. More expensive, but reliable and predictable.

3. **Universal Life Insurance**: A flexible form of permanent insurance that allows you to adjust premiums and death benefits. Cash value accumulates based on interest rates.

4. **Second-to-Die (Survivorship) Insurance**: Covers two people—usually both parents—and pays out after the second person dies. Often used in special needs planning because the need

for funds often arises only after both parents are gone. These policies are usually more affordable than two individual policies and work well for funding a special needs trust.

Determining the Right Amount of Coverage

How much life insurance is enough? The answer depends largely on your current stage of life and your planning priorities.

If you're still raising children at home, consider how much coverage would be needed to replace the income of the working parent in the event of their death to help maintain your household's financial stability. A common benchmark is 10 to 15 times your annual income, though individual needs will vary.

For families no longer in that caregiving stage, the calculation may shift toward how much you want to leave behind—particularly for a child with special needs. This involves subtracting anticipated resources, such as government benefits and assets already designated in a special needs trust, from your overall legacy goals.

Be sure to also consider future support for other children or charitable giving, if those are part of your long-term vision. A well-thought-out plan reflects not just current needs, but the broader legacy you want to leave.

Avoiding a Common Mistake: The Beneficiary Designation

One of the most critical rules in special needs planning is this: never name your child with disabilities as the direct beneficiary of your life insurance policy. Doing so could disqualify them from receiving essential government benefits, which often have strict asset limits.

Instead, your policy should name a third-party special needs trust as the beneficiary. This ensures the funds are held and managed in a way that supplements government support rather than replacing it or causing your child to lose access to it. The trust can then distribute funds for education, therapies, caregivers, travel, recreation, and other "non-essential" quality-of-life expenses without jeopardizing benefits.

Overcoming Health Concerns and Budget Limits

Parents sometimes hesitate to apply for life insurance because of existing health conditions or tight budgets. Fortunately, there are options for nearly every situation:

- **Guaranteed Issue Policies**: Available without medical exams, though typically limited in coverage and more expensive.
- **Group Policies**: Often offered through employers with relaxed underwriting and affordable premiums.
- **Simplified Underwriting**: A middle ground for those who may not qualify for fully underwritten policies but still want a reasonable level of coverage.

The key is to apply sooner rather than later—premiums increase with age and declining health. Even a modest policy can make a significant difference.

A Tool for Generational Planning

Life insurance is also a tool for managing broader family dynamics. For example:

- If you plan to leave the majority of your estate to a special needs trust, a life insurance policy can provide **an equal inheritance to other children**.
- It can create a **legacy for charitable causes** or fund a foundation to support your child and others with similar needs.
- It can provide **liquidity for estate taxes or legal fees,** particularly if your estate includes illiquid assets like a home or business.

What makes life insurance uniquely valuable is its ability to create an *"instant estate."* A relatively small monthly premium can translate into hundreds of thousands of dollars available at the exact moment it's needed. For many families who may not have significant wealth built up, this can be a game-changer in securing their child's future.

Imagine paying $50–$100 per month and knowing that, should the unthinkable happen, your beneficiary will immediately receive a $500,000 benefit. That's the kind of financial power and peace of mind life insurance provides.

When Life Insurance and Special Needs Trusts Work Together

The most effective use of life insurance in special needs planning comes when it is directly integrated with your overall estate and financial strategy. The process typically looks like this:

1. You establish a **special needs trust**.
2. You purchase a **life insurance policy** with the trust named as the beneficiary.
3. Upon your passing, the death benefit is paid directly into the trust.
4. The trustee manages those funds in accordance with your instructions, supporting your child's needs for decades to come.

This integration ensures continuity of care, benefit protection, and responsible management of resources.

Final Thoughts: The Peace of Mind You Deserve

Life insurance isn't just a financial product—it's a plan for love, stability, and continuity. For special needs families, it's a lifeline that makes your values and intentions real long after you're gone.

By choosing the right type of policy, determining the appropriate amount of coverage, and coordinating it with a properly structured special needs trust, you're doing more than protecting your family financially. You're preserving a way of life. You're empowering loved ones to continue receiving the care they deserve, surrounded by the supports you carefully arranged.

This isn't about fear—it's about **confidence**. Confidence that you've done everything in your power to prepare for whatever lies ahead. And confidence that, no matter what the future holds, your child will have the resources, protection, and love you worked so hard to secure.

Life Insurance at a Glance: Comparing Key Policy Types

	Term Life	Whole Life	Universal Life	Second-to-Die
Coverage Duration	Temporary	Lifelong	Lifelong	Until second death
Premium	Fixed for the term; lowest cost	Fixed and higher cost	Flexible (can adjust over time)	Usually lower than insuring two lives separately
Cash Value	None	Yes - grows at a guaranteed rate	Yes - grows based on interest	Yes - may accumulate value depending on structure
Flexibility for Policy Holder	Low - expires if not renewed	Low - predictable but inflexible	High - can adjust premiums and death benefit	Low - designed for estate planning, not flexibility
Payout Timing	Upon death during the term	Guaranteed when insured dies	Guaranteed when insured dies	Paid after both insured individuals pass away

Chapter Seven

Expense Considerations for Education & Schooling

More Than Just a School Decision

We moved to a new town in 2020—arguably one of the hardest times to transition a child who thrives on routine and relationships. We enrolled in the local public school system, but, after just a few months, we hit a wall.

Try doing occupational therapy with a visually impaired child over Zoom. It wasn't effective—and while I truly commend the school's efforts during an impossible time, it was clear that school, already a challenge, had just become even harder. Our son began taking steps backward as he struggled to adjust to new people, a new building (even when they were in-seat), and constantly shifting routines. He started fixating on how many students were there each day, which only added to his social anxiety, and eventually began resisting even entering the classroom.

Because he was new to the district, the staff wanted to conduct their own evaluations. Soon, conversations started circling around a specialized classroom placement. I don't think I wear rose-colored glasses—but, deep down, I knew this wasn't where our son needed to be.

I remember sitting in the car after another difficult meeting, staring at the steering wheel, knowing deep down that we'd probably need to look elsewhere. And that meant cost—tuition, transportation, therapies the school wouldn't cover. We had just moved him the year before. He had only ever known public school. It was the system I had taught in. It was the system I understood. And we didn't know how we were going to pay for private school. It was scary. Were we about to make a move in the wrong direction?

But something in my gut told me we couldn't ignore what wasn't working. Our son needed something different. He needed an environment that wouldn't just try to keep him afloat—but one that would help him thrive.

Our decision to consider private school wasn't about prestige or status. It was about genuinely finding the best learning environment. We toured schools, asked hard questions, and did our due diligence. Some schools even *"deselected"* us along the way. But eventually, we found a small school rooted in competency-based learning. It was beautiful—especially for a child with areas of brilliance alongside areas of needed growth.

As a former educator, I knew that regardless of whether a child attends public or private school, the local district is still responsible for offering certain services. So I advocated. Eventually, though, we chose not to use those services—not because he didn't need them, but because they disrupted his day more than they helped.

Instead, we turned to private clinics for PT, OT, and speech—and, over time, something amazing happened. I built strong relationships with those therapists, and, in collaboration with the school, we created an alliance. Our son's outpatient therapists began providing services at the school during the day. It was a huge win: we were able to maintain consistent, quality therapy in a real-world setting, and we reclaimed a few precious evening hours as a family.

In the end, we made the choice to move forward with private education—and we've made sacrifices to afford it. We've had to get creative, juggle priorities, and search for every available resource, credit, and workaround to make it work.

It's not a decision we take lightly. But for us, it was never just about picking a school—it was about choosing a place where his potential could be nurtured and protected.

~Ashli
EAVES

Breaking Down the Mountain: One Step at a Time

Navigating your child's educational future isn't about solving everything today—it's about building a path forward, one informed step at a time. For parents of children with special needs, the education system can feel especially complex, filled with unfamiliar terminology, evolving laws, and decisions that impact not just the present but years down the road. Add in the everyday demands of caregiving and professional responsibilities, and it's easy to feel overwhelmed before the journey even begins.

The key isn't having all the answers up front. Instead, it's adopting a strategy of thoughtful progression—breaking big, emotional decisions into smaller, manageable actions. This approach helps families make steady, confident progress without getting stuck in the uncertainty. For high-earning professionals in particular, a structured, step-by-step process is helpful. It allows them to balance their careers with the additional demands of special needs parenting, all while laying the groundwork for a more secure educational and financial future.

For many families, education expenses represent one of the largest financial commitments they'll make for their child with special needs. The costs can vary dramatically depending on whether you choose public or private education, specialized programs, or supplemental therapies. Adding to this complexity is the potential to classify certain educational expenses as medical costs for tax purposes, or to access specialized funding streams like Education Savings Accounts (ESAs) in states such as Missouri. Each option carries different financial implications that must be carefully evaluated against your child's specific needs.

The Power of Incremental Decision-Making

When parents try to make all educational funding decisions simultaneously, crucial details often fall through the cracks. The pressure to "get it right" can lead to decision paralysis or hasty choices that don't align with long-term goals. **A staged approach allows for thorough research and consideration at each step**, reducing the likelihood of costly mistakes or oversights. This doesn't mean postponing important decisions; rather, it means tackling them in a logical sequence that builds toward a comprehensive plan.

What makes this incremental approach particularly effective is how it accommodates the evolving nature of your child's needs. A financial strategy created when your child is in elementary school will likely need adjustments as they progress to middle school, high school, and potentially post-secondary education. By establishing a framework of regular review points, you create natural opportunities to reassess and refine your approach without feeling overwhelmed by constant decision-making.

The following sections of this chapter will guide you through three critical aspects of education funding for your special needs child. First, we'll explore the financial considerations when choosing between public and private educational settings, comparing not just the obvious tuition differences but also the hidden costs and potential funding sources for each option. Next, we'll clarify when and how educational expenses might qualify as medical expenses for tax purposes. Finally, we'll examine specialized funding mechanisms and other education funding options that may be available to support your child's educational journey.

By approaching these considerations methodically and incrementally, you'll build confidence in your decisions while creating a financial blueprint that truly serves your child's educational needs. Remember that thoroughness, not speed, is your ally in this process. Each step you take builds upon the last, creating a foundation of knowledge and action that will support your family for years to come.

Navigating the Educational Landscape

Choosing the right educational path for a child with special needs involves careful consideration of both financial and educational factors. Public and private schools offer distinct advantages and drawbacks that parents must weigh against their child's specific needs and the family's financial situation.

Public schools, funded and operated by local districts, are required under federal law (IDEA—the Individuals with Disabilities Education

Act) to provide a Free Appropriate Public Education (FAPE) in the Least Restrictive Environment (LRE). This means public schools must evaluate your child, create an Individualized Education Plan (IEP) if they qualify, and deliver services such as speech therapy, occupational therapy, or specialized instruction—at no cost to the family.

The benefits of public school often include access to a wide range of related services, specialized staff, and legal protections. However, parents may encounter challenges like overcrowded classrooms, inconsistencies in implementation, or limited flexibility in curriculum. Some schools excel in special education; others may be under-resourced or lack training in more complex needs.

Private schools vary widely in their structure, philosophy, and resources. Some are general education institutions, while others specialize in learning differences, autism, or methodologies. Since private schools aren't bound by IDEA, they aren't required to offer IEPs or provide services unless they receive public funding. However, what they *do* offer can be highly tailored—smaller class sizes, specialized teaching methods, and a learning environment that may better fit your child's personality or learning style.

The downsides? Private education is typically tuition-based, and services like therapy or academic support may be billed separately. As of the 2024–2025 academic year, average private school tuition in the United States ranges from $13,000 to over $37,000 annually. Specialized programs that support children with developmental, behavioral, or learning differences often fall at the higher end—or even exceed—this range due to the need for tailored instruction, therapeutic services, and low student-to-teacher ratios. Not all private schools are equipped to handle complex or high-needs disabilities. Additionally, there's no legal obligation for them to admit or accommodate a student with special needs unless it aligns with their mission.

So, how do you decide? Start by thinking beyond labels and focus on fit. Tour schools. Talk to staff. Observe classrooms. And most importantly, trust your instincts. Your child deserves a setting where they are not only supported—but seen, challenged, and celebrated.

What Happens to My Child's IEP If We Choose a Private School?

Parents often wonder what supports are still available if they opt to place their child in a private school—even when the child already has an Individualized Education Plan (IEP) through the public school district. The answer lies in the difference between a public placement and a parental placement.

If your child is placed in a private school by the public school district because they could not meet the child's needs appropriately, the district is generally responsible for the cost and must continue to provide special education services under IDEA. However, if you choose to place your child in a private school—known as a parental placement—the rules shift.

In this case, your child no longer has an enforceable right to the full range of services guaranteed under IDEA. However, under Equitable Services provisions, your local public school district is still required to consult with private school representatives and offer a proportionate share of services to students with disabilities who attend private schools within the district's boundaries.

Instead of an IEP, the district may develop a Service Plan that outlines what supports will be provided—if any. These services are often more limited than those offered under a public IEP and might include only specific types of therapy, consultation, or part-time support. It's also important to note that the school district decides what services to offer and is not required to provide transportation or implement the entire IEP in the private setting.

That said, families still have rights. You can request an evaluation or reevaluation through the public district while your child is in private school. And if you believe the district failed to provide FAPE in a public setting and you were forced to move your child to a private program, you may be able to seek reimbursement through due process—but that's a legal step and not guaranteed.

In short, enrolling in a private school doesn't necessarily eliminate access to public school support, but it does meaningfully alter what services your child may be eligible to receive. It's essential to understand the difference and speak directly with your local district's special education coordinator when weighing this decision.

School Selection Checklist for Parents

Use this list to help clarify your family's priorities and guide your school exploration process:

- What are my child's specific learning, social, and behavioral needs?
- Does the school offer services that match my child's IEP or diagnosis?
- How experienced is the staff in working with children with similar

challenges?

- What is the average class size and student-to-teacher ratio?
- Is there access to in-house therapies (speech, OT, PT, counseling)?
- Does the school have a behavior plan or inclusion philosophy?
- How does the school handle bullying or emotional safety?
- What does a typical day look like for a student in my child's grade or program?
- Are parents considered part of the educational team?
- What is the school's communication style and frequency?
- For private schools: What is the total cost, including tuition, therapies, and materials?
- Are there scholarships, 529, or ABLE-compatible ways to help fund tuition?
- Is transportation provided or feasible for our family?
- What does my gut tell me after visiting or talking to current families?

Beyond tuition, families should consider additional costs when comparing educational options. These might include transportation, specialized therapies not covered by the school, assistive technology, and supplementary educational materials. Public schools may provide some of these services as part of an IEP, while private school families might need to arrange and pay for them separately.

The decision between public and private education isn't just financial—it's deeply personal. Some families find that their local public school offers excellent special education services in an inclusive environment. Others discover that a private setting better addresses their child's specific learning style or provides a community where they thrive socially and emotionally.

When comparing educational settings, the best financial decision integrates both immediate costs and long-term value, considering not just dollar amounts but the quality of educational outcomes for your unique child.

When Education Becomes Medicine

The intersection of education and healthcare is particularly significant for children with special needs. In certain circumstances, educational expenses can qualify as medical expenses for tax purposes, offering families potential financial relief through tax deductions or savings accounts.

According to the Internal Revenue Service (IRS), tuition for a school that primarily provides medical care or special education for children with disabilities may qualify as a medical expense. This classification depends on the recommendation of a medical practitioner and the primary purpose of the program or school. For an expense to qualify, the principal reason for choosing the school must be its specialized resources that address the child's medical needs—not merely educational preferences.

Think about it this way: just as a doctor might prescribe medication or physical therapy to treat a medical condition, they might also prescribe a specific educational environment or approach. When education functions as treatment—directly addressing conditions like autism, learning disabilities, or emotional disorders—the line between education and healthcare blurs. The classroom becomes a treatment space, and teachers serve alongside therapists as part of the care team.

To claim educational expenses as medical deductions, families need proper documentation. This typically includes a letter from a physician or other healthcare provider explicitly recommending the special education services as part of the child's treatment plan. The letter should detail the medical condition and explain why the particular educational setting or service is medically necessary. Maintaining organized records of all related costs, including tuition, fees, and specialized materials, is essential for substantiating these claims during tax filing.

Medical expenses, including qualifying educational costs, may be deductible if they exceed 7.5% of your adjusted gross income and you itemize deductions on your tax return. For many families of children with special needs, this threshold is achievable given the various therapies, specialized equipment, and educational services their children require. However, the recent increase in the standard deduction under tax law changes means fewer taxpayers benefit from itemizing, potentially limiting the value of this deduction for some families.

Beyond tax deductions, families may be able to use Health Savings Accounts (HSAs) or Flexible Spending Accounts (FSAs) to pay for **qualified medical expenses** that support a child's education—such as speech therapy, occupational therapy, psychological services, or certain diagnostic evaluations. These expenses often overlap with educational needs for children with disabilities, especially when therapies are part of an IEP or recommended by a medical provider.

Using pre-tax dollars from an HSA or FSA can result in significant savings by lowering your taxable income. For example, a family in the 24% tax bracket could save $2,400 on $10,000 of qualified medical expenses paid through an HSA. While these accounts don't cover tuition or general education costs, they can still offer meaningful tax advantages for families managing multiple therapy or intervention-related expenses

Community resources can also help offset the cost of medically necessary education. Local non-profit organizations, foundations focused on specific disabilities, and community grant programs sometimes provide financial assistance for specialized educational services. While these resources may not cover all expenses, they can complement other funding strategies to make comprehensive care more affordable.

The key to successfully navigating this complex landscape lies in detailed planning and record-keeping. Families should develop a system for tracking all education-related expenses that might qualify as medical costs. Digital tools, dedicated folders for receipts and medical recommendations, and regular consultation with tax professionals who specialize in special needs planning can make this process more manageable.

How might reframing your child's educational needs as part of their medical care open new pathways to financial support and tax savings?

Maximizing Educational Funding Resources

Education Savings Accounts (ESAs) in Missouri represent a powerful tool for families seeking to customize their child's educational experience. These state-funded accounts provide qualifying students with funds that can be used for a variety of educational expenses. The Missouri Empowerment Scholarship Accounts Program, established in 2021, allows eligible students to receive funds that can be directed toward private school tuition, online learning programs, tutoring services, educational therapies, and more.

Qualification for Missouri's ESA program centers primarily on students with disabilities or those from low-income families. The application process requires documentation of eligibility, proof of Missouri residency, and sometimes evidence of the student's specific educational needs. Families are required to submit expense reports showing how the money has been used for qualified educational purposes. This accountability ensures the program serves its intended purpose while giving families flexibility in tailoring education to their child's needs.

Using ESA funds effectively requires strategic planning. Many families find success by mapping out their child's educational needs for the entire school year, prioritizing expenses based on impact and necessity. This approach is similar to creating a household budget, where limited resources must be allocated thoughtfully across various needs. Just as you might prioritize essential utilities before entertainment expenses in your home budget, you might allocate ESA funds to critical therapies or core academic services before supplementary programs.

It's also important to understand that not all private schools qualify for or participate in the MOScholars program. To receive funds, schools must be approved by the state and meet specific criteria outlined by the Missouri State Treasurer's office. Even among eligible schools, some may choose not to accept MOScholars scholarships due to internal policies or capacity constraints. Before assuming funds can be used at a particular school, be sure to confirm the school's participation and discuss any requirements they may have for enrollment or continued eligibility.

Many private organizations offer grants and scholarships specifically for students with disabilities. Organizations like the National Center for Learning Disabilities, the United Cerebral Palsy Association, and various autism-focused foundations provide financial assistance for educational expenses. Additionally, disability-specific organizations often maintain lists of scholarship opportunities relevant to particular conditions. These funding sources typically require applications detailing the student's needs, educational goals, and financial circumstances.

Tax credits offer yet another avenue for managing educational expenses. The American Opportunity Tax Credit provides up to $2,500 per eligible student for qualified education expenses, while the Lifetime Learning Credit offers up to $2,000 per tax return. While these credits typically apply to postsecondary education, families should consult with tax professionals about their applicability to specialized programs for students with disabilities, as some may qualify under specific circumstances.

Special needs trusts present another avenue for managing educational expenses. These legal arrangements allow assets to be set aside for the benefit of a person with disabilities without affecting their eligibility for government benefits. Trustees can use trust funds to pay for educational services that enhance the beneficiary's quality of life but aren't covered by public programs. This approach provides both financial support and protection of valuable benefits like Medicaid and Supplemental Security Income.

Strategic Use of 529 and ABLE Accounts in Special Needs Planning

For families navigating the costs of education and long-term care for a child with special needs, understanding how to maximize tax-advantaged accounts is essential. Two tools often used in tandem—529 education savings plans and ABLE accounts—offer unique benefits. However, knowing how and when to use them together can make all the difference in both maximizing opportunity and preserving government benefit eligibility.

Understanding the Tools

529 Education Savings Plans are state-sponsored accounts designed to help families save for educational expenses in a tax-advantaged way. Contributions grow tax-deferred, and withdrawals used for qualified education expenses—such as tuition, fees, books, and now up to $10,000 annually for K-12 private school tuition—are tax-free. This expanded use, thanks to the 2017 Tax Cuts and Jobs Act, has made 529 plans especially valuable for families seeking specialized private education during elementary and high school years.

ABLE Accounts, established under the Achieving a Better Life Experience (ABLE) Act, are designed specifically for individuals with disabilities.

Contributions to ABLE accounts also grow tax-deferred, and withdrawals used for qualified disability-related expenses are tax-free. Unlike 529 plans, ABLE accounts offer an added layer of protection: assets held in an ABLE account do not count toward the $2,000 asset limit that can affect eligibility for benefits such as Supplemental Security Income (SSI) and Medicaid—as long as the account balance remains below $100,000.

When It Makes Sense to Use Both

Used together strategically, 529 and ABLE accounts can serve different but complementary roles:

- **Education and Beyond**: A 529 plan is ideal for planning specifically around educational costs, including specialized programs that a child with special needs might require. Meanwhile, an ABLE account can cover broader, lifelong disability-related expenses such as housing, transportation, therapies, and assistive technology.

- **Preserving Benefits**: If a child is nearing adulthood or is already receiving SSI, it becomes increasingly important to manage account ownership carefully. Since a 529 plan is typically owned by the parent, it does not count toward the child's asset limit. However, funds withdrawn from a 529 and handed directly to the child could be considered income, potentially affecting SSI. This is where the ABLE account becomes crucial. Rolling funds from a 529 into an ABLE account (up to the annual limit—$19,000 in 2025) can allow the money to be used in a benefit-safe way for qualified expenses.

- **Rollover Strategy**: The IRS allows tax-free rollovers from a 529 plan into an ABLE account for the same beneficiary (or a qualifying family member), up to the ABLE contribution limit. This flexibility allows families to shift unused 529 funds into an ABLE account if educational needs change or if there's a surplus in the 529 plan.

When Using Both May Not Make Sense

While the 529-to-ABLE rollover can be a powerful tactic, it's not always the best move:

- **Short-Term Needs vs. Long-Term Growth**: If funds are needed in the short term for education-related expenses, it may be more efficient to use the 529 plan directly rather than transferring to an ABLE account and potentially limiting access to the money through ABLE-specific qualified expenses.

- **Contribution Limits**: The annual ABLE contribution cap—$19,000 for 2025—can limit how much can be rolled over from a 529 in a single year. If a family needs to move more than that in a short timeframe, it may take multiple years or alternative strategies to reposition the funds.

- **Investment Choices and Fees**: Investment options within ABLE and 529 plans vary by state and may differ in performance or cost. Families should compare these carefully before consolidating or rolling over funds.

- **Redundancy**: If a child is not expected to need ongoing disability-related financial support—or if long-term government benefit eligibility is unlikely to be an issue—an ABLE account may offer limited value compared to more flexible options like a trust.

Planning Tip

For families of children with disabilities, one of the smartest approaches is to use a 529 plan during the early years for education-focused goals and then transition any unused or excess funds into an ABLE account as the child nears adulthood. This ensures optimal tax treatment, preserves eligibility for essential programs, and creates a bridge from education into lifelong support.

Comparison of 529 Plans and ABLE Accounts

529 Plan	ABLE Account
Tax deferred growth; tax-free withdrawals for qualified expenses	Tax deferred growth; tax-free withdrawals for qualified expenses
Focus on education	Focus on disability-related needs, can also include education
Qualified Expenses: can include education-related expenses; focus on tuition, books, fees	Qualified Expenses: Can include things such as housing, transportation, healthcare, therapy, etc. in addition to education-related expenses
Can be owned by a parent or guardian; Usually owned by parent	Owned by beneficiary with parent or guardian that acts as authorized representative on the account; Can also be owned by parent or guardian
Parent-owned 529s do not impact SSI/Medicaid	Does not impact SSI/Medicaid benefits if under $100,000; has built in protection for benefit eligibility
Subject to annual contribution limits; Lifetime limits vary by state	Subject to annual contribution limits; Lifetime limits vary by state
Can roll a 529 to another 529 or to an ABLE (counts as contribution for that year)	ABLE cannot roll to 529
Eligible beneficiary does not have age/disability limit	Eligible beneficiary must have disability onset before age 26 (or 46 under SECURE 2.0)

Educational funding for children with special needs doesn't rely on a single source, but rather a carefully constructed financial strategy that draws from public programs, tax advantages, private scholarships, and personal savings. By breaking down the complex funding landscape into manageable components—comparing public and private options, identifying qualifying medical expenses, and maximizing available financial resources—families can create comprehensive educational plans that address their child's needs without overwhelming their finances. This incremental approach to educational planning reflects the broader philosophy of tackling special needs financial planning in stages rather than attempting to solve everything at once.

Taking the Next Step in Your Child's Educational Planning

Throughout this chapter, we've broken down complex funding structures, expense classifications, and resource options into digestible segments that allow you to build your knowledge incrementally rather than tackling everything at once.

When facing educational decisions for your child, it's easy to feel pulled in multiple directions. You might wonder if you should invest in private education, how to secure appropriate funding, or whether certain expenses qualify for tax benefits. The weight of these choices can feel immense, especially when balanced against your professional responsibilities and day-to-day caregiving.

Education Planning is an ongoing process that evolves with your child. The knowledge you've gained about funding options and expense classifications gives you tools to adapt as circumstances change. You're now equipped to make informed choices about educational settings while maximizing available financial resources.

As high-achieving professionals who also serve as caregivers, your time is precious. The structured approach outlined in this chapter helps you make progress in brief, focused sessions rather than requiring lengthy blocks of uninterrupted time that rarely materialize in your busy schedule.

By applying this incremental strategy to your educational planning, you're not just organizing finances—you're creating space to focus on what truly matters: finding the educational environment where your child can thrive. When financial considerations are methodically addressed, you gain the clarity needed to advocate effectively for your child's educational needs.

As we move forward to the next chapter, carry this approach with you. The habit of breaking complex challenges into manageable steps will serve you well throughout your financial planning journey, bringing order to what once seemed overwhelming and giving you confidence in the path ahead.

Chapter Eight

Other Tax Considerations & Write-Offs

The Miles, the Meals, and the Missed Deductions

For years, I did our taxes myself—just me, some software, and a quiet weekend carved out to get it done. It wasn't something I looked forward to, but it felt manageable... until it didn't.

After our son's diagnosis, everything started to feel more complicated. There were therapy bills, medical expenses, evaluations, and so many appointments. I remember sitting there, staring at my computer, wondering how I was supposed to capture the full picture of our life in a series of tax forms. I was always questioning whether I was missing something, an opportunity to give us a little relief given our additional expenses. I was also always questioning if I was doing it right.

Eventually, I reached a point where I knew I couldn't do it alone anymore. We started working with a CPA, and I walked into that first meeting feeling a little embarrassed—like I should've had it all figured out.

Now, as a business owner, my financial world has even more layers. Retirement planning, quarterly estimates, write-offs—it's a lot to think through. Having professional help isn't just a convenience anymore; it's a necessity. But what's changed even more is my mindset. I don't see tax planning as a burden or an afterthought—I see it as part of the broader plan to care for our family.

As I learned more—especially after earning the Chartered Special Needs Consultant (ChSNC) designation—I began to recognize opportunities we'd overlooked. I started asking better questions. I stopped assuming we were ineligible just because something seemed too technical or complicated.

And, slowly, there were small wins. Tax credits we didn't know applied to us. Medical deductions we'd never claimed. Things that seemed minor, but, in the midst of everything else, those little pieces of relief mattered.

Now we track everything. We ask better questions. We keep records we used to throw away. Because the tax code isn't designed with our life in mind—but that doesn't mean we can't learn to use it to our advantage.

~Ashli
EAVES

Beyond the Basics: Tax Strategies That Create Financial Breathing Room

While earlier chapters have addressed the foundational aspects of a financial plan, this chapter focuses on an often overlooked but critically important component: tax considerations and strategic write-offs. For families supporting children with special needs, **tax planning isn't**

merely about compliance—it's about maximizing every available resource.

The financial landscape for special needs families is constantly shifting. Medical advancements, educational innovations, legal reforms, and economic fluctuations all impact the effectiveness of even the most carefully constructed financial plans. This dynamic environment demands an equally dynamic approach to financial planning—one that recognizes the importance of regular reviews and thoughtful adjustments to ensure your strategies remain aligned with your child's evolving needs and your family's changing circumstances.

Too often, families invest significant time and resources in creating initial financial and legal arrangements, only to let these plans gather dust. **A static financial plan, however well-intentioned, can gradually lose its effectiveness** as your child grows, as their needs change, and as the regulatory landscape evolves. This chapter advocates for a more responsive approach—one that treats financial planning as an ongoing process rather than a one-time event.

Tax planning represents a perfect example of this necessary flexibility. The tax advantages available to families with special needs children are substantial but often underutilized. From medical expense deductions to education credits, from therapy cost write-offs to specialized equipment deductions, the tax code offers numerous provisions that can significantly reduce your annual tax burden. These savings, when strategically reinvested, can strengthen your child's long-term financial security.

In the pages that follow, we'll explore three key areas of tax planning that deserve your attention. First, we'll examine the range of tax deductions and credits specifically designed for families with special needs children, helping you identify which ones apply to your situation. Next, we'll clarify which medical expenses, therapy costs, and related expenditures qualify as legitimate tax write-offs, providing guidance on documentation requirements and claiming procedures. Finally, we'll introduce strategies for year-round tax planning that can help you maximize these benefits consistently.

Think of these tax benefits like revisiting a familiar city and uncovering charming side streets and hidden cafés you missed the first time around—discoveries that not only surprise you but also enhance the entire experience. There's often more available than initially apparent—if you know where to look.

The goal isn't merely to reduce your tax bill—though that's certainly a welcome outcome. Rather, **the true objective is to be more efficient with your finances to relieve current financial pressures and save money that can be directed toward your family's current obligations or future planning of your child's care.** Every dollar saved through strategic tax planning is a dollar that can be invested in your child's special needs trust, used for current therapies, or set aside for future care requirements. This approach transforms tax planning from a dreaded annual chore into a powerful tool within your comprehensive financial blueprint.

This chapter serves as your practical guide to navigating these tax considerations, offering clear explanations and actionable steps rather than abstract theories. By implementing these strategies and committing to regular reviews of your financial plans, you'll enhance your ability to provide for your child's unique needs—today and for years to come.

Understanding Tax Credits for Special Needs Families

Navigating the tax landscape as a parent of a child with special needs can seem daunting. Yet, knowing which tax benefits apply to your situation can significantly reduce your annual tax burden. The Internal Revenue Service (IRS) offers various deductions and credits specifically designed for families who have dependents with disabilities or special needs.

Tax credits work differently than a deduction. While a deduction reduces your taxable income, a credit directly reduces your tax bill dollar for dollar. It's like the difference between a discount on an item's price versus receiving cash back after your purchase. Credits typically provide greater savings than deductions of the same amount

The Child Tax Credit provides up to $2,000 per qualifying child under age 17, with a portion of it potentially refundable depending on income. However, this credit generally phases out after age 17—even if your child has special needs. There is no special exception for children with disabilities in terms of age eligibility, but families may be able to shift to the Other Dependent Credit once their child no longer qualifies for the CTC.

When a child no longer qualifies for the Child Tax Credit—typically after age 17—you may still be eligible for a nonrefundable credit of up to $500 through the Other Dependent Credit. If your child has a permanent disability, you may continue to claim them as a dependent regardless of age, allowing you to receive this credit in future years. It's a small benefit, but one that adds up over time for lifelong caregiving situations.

The Dependent Care Credit helps cover a portion of work-related child care expenses. While this typically applies to children under 13, **there's**

an exception for dependents of any age who are physically or mentally incapable of self-care. That means parents of children with special needs—even teenagers or adults—can still claim the credit for qualifying care expenses that allow them to work or look for work. Eligible expenses may include after-school programs, day programs, or specialized care providers.

Some families may also qualify for the Earned Income Tax Credit (EITC), which benefits low to moderate income working individuals and families. If you have a qualifying child with a disability, the age restrictions for this credit don't apply. This means you could continue to receive this valuable credit even after your child turns 19.

Understanding and claiming all applicable tax benefits can save special needs families thousands of dollars annually, creating more financial resources to support their child's care and future planning needs.

Maximizing Medical and Therapy Tax Deductions

The medical expense deduction can offer meaningful tax relief for families supporting a child with special needs—especially when out-of-pocket costs are high. Under current tax law, if you itemize deductions, you may be able to deduct qualified medical expenses that exceed **7.5% of your adjusted gross income (AGI)**. For many families in this situation, reaching that threshold is not uncommon due to the ongoing costs of care.

Eligible expenses go beyond routine medical visits. They may include therapy sessions, hospital stays, specialized equipment, and certain home modifications made for medical reasons. In some cases, tuition for special education, transportation to medical appointments, and even costs associated with a trained service animal may also qualify. Because these types of expenses can add up quickly, the medical expense deduction remains one of the more valuable tax planning opportunities available to families in the special needs community—provided the requirements are met.

If you plan to deduct medical expenses, **start tracking them now—not at tax time**. Waiting until the last minute often leads to missing receipts or incomplete records. The IRS requires detailed documentation, including dates, amounts, providers, and the nature of each expense. For items that could be seen as personal rather than medical—like adaptive equipment or special schooling—a letter of medical necessity from your child's doctor can help substantiate the claim. Setting up a system to organize receipts, insurance statements, and payment records throughout the year—whether in a binder or with a digital app—can make the process more manageable and provide peace of mind if you're ever audited.

Transportation costs related to medical care often go unclaimed, yet they can represent a valuable deduction. The IRS allows you to deduct expenses for traveling to and from medical appointments, therapy sessions, and specialized treatments. You can choose between deducting actual costs (gas, oil, parking fees, tolls) or using the standard medical mileage rate. For families making frequent trips to specialists or therapy centers, these costs accumulate significantly over a year.

Education-related expenses pose particular complexity for special needs tax planning. Regular education costs typically aren't deductible, but special education necessitated by a child's disability often qualifies as a medical expense. This may include tuition for schools providing medical care or special needs instruction, tutoring recommended by a doctor, and certain learning disability programs. The key determining factor is whether the program or service primarily addresses your child's medical needs rather than providing general education. Not every educational expense will qualify, but those directed specifically at addressing your child's medical condition often do. A neuropsychological evaluation that identifies learning disabilities, for instance, may qualify as a medical expense, as might specialized reading programs recommended by doctors to address those specific disabilities.

Assistive technology represents another significant deduction category. Devices that compensate for a physical or mental disability—such as communication devices, modified computers, mobility aids, or sensory integration equipment—generally qualify as deductible medical expenses. Even seemingly ordinary items can qualify if they're specially designed for disability needs, such as specialized car seats, adaptive clothing, or therapeutic toys recommended by medical professionals.

Insurance premiums you pay for policies covering medical care are typically deductible. This includes premiums for health insurance, long-term care insurance, and specialized medical policies if you pay these costs with after-tax dollars. However, insurance premiums paid through an employer's pre-tax plan don't qualify since they're already tax-advantaged.

How could strategic timing of medical expenses further reduce your tax burden, potentially concentrating deductible expenses in alternating years to exceed the 7.5% threshold more substantially?

Strategic Tax Planning for Special Needs Families

Tax planning shouldn't be a once-a-year scramble. For families supporting children with special needs, adopting a proactive, year-round approach can maximize tax advantages and significantly reduce your overall tax burden. Strategic planning allows you to time expenses, leverage tax-advantaged accounts, and coordinate benefits to optimize your financial situation.

Consider implementing a *"bunching"* strategy for medical expenses. Since you can only deduct medical costs that exceed 7.5% of your adjusted gross income, concentrating larger medical purchases or elective procedures in alternate years may help you surpass this threshold more substantially. For example, if you know your child needs specialized equipment or multiple therapies, scheduling these in the same tax year might generate enough expenses to qualify for the deduction, while spreading them across two years might result in no deduction at all.

Flexible Spending Accounts (FSAs) and Health Savings Accounts (HSAs) offer powerful tax advantages for medical expenses. FSAs, available through many employers, allow you to set aside pre-tax dollars for qualified medical expenses, effectively saving you the equivalent of your tax rate on these costs. HSAs, available to those with high-deductible health plans, provide a triple tax advantage: tax-deductible contributions, tax-free growth, and tax-free withdrawals for qualified medical expenses. For families with predictable medical needs, making the most of these accounts should be a central part of your tax planning strategy.

Dependent Care FSAs present another tax-saving opportunity. These accounts allow you to set aside up to $5,000 pre-tax for qualifying dependent care expenses that enable you to work or look for work.

For children with special needs, this might include specialized daycare, after-school programs, or certain therapeutic activities. Using a Dependent Care FSA can generate tax savings of $1,000 to $2,000 annually, depending on your tax bracket.

ABLE accounts represent one of the most significant tax planning tools specifically designed for disability expenses. Contributions aren't tax-deductible federally (though some states offer deductions), but earnings grow tax-free when used for qualified disability expenses. ABLE accounts can hold up to $100,000 without impacting SSI benefits, making them valuable components of a comprehensive tax strategy.

Strategic tax planning requires year-round attention and coordination between various tax benefits, medical expenses, and specialized accounts. By understanding available deductions, timing expenses strategically, and utilizing tax-advantaged accounts like FSAs, HSAs, and ABLE accounts, families can significantly reduce their tax burden while maximizing resources available for their child's care and future planning needs.

Bringing It All Together

Effective special needs financial planning isn't just about saving and investing—it's about understanding how all the moving parts fit together. And few areas are as powerful or as often overlooked as tax planning. When done thoughtfully, tax planning becomes more than a once-a-year activity—it becomes a consistent, strategic effort to preserve resources and create long-term financial flexibility for your family.

This chapter has highlighted several important tools: tax credits, medical expense deductions, and tax-advantaged accounts like ABLE accounts. While each offers its own set of benefits, they're most effective when coordinated. The key is to approach them not as isolated opportunities, but as interconnected pieces of your overall strategy. For example, the timing of medical procedures, careful tracking of qualified expenses, and proactive contributions to eligible accounts can turn routine costs into tax-efficient opportunities.

That said, navigating the nuances of tax law—especially as it intersects with government benefits—requires expertise. A financial advisor familiar with special needs planning, paired with a knowledgeable tax professional, can help you uncover overlooked opportunities and avoid missteps that could impact eligibility or long-term plans. This team-based approach ensures your strategy remains aligned with current regulations and your evolving family goals.

Just as your child's needs change over time, so should your financial and tax planning. Therapeutic costs, educational programs, and benefit eligibility can shift as your child moves from childhood to adulthood. Similarly, tax rules can evolve. That's why reviewing your strategy at least twice a year is more than a good habit—it's a critical part of maintaining a responsive and sustainable plan.

With the insights you've gained in this chapter, you're better prepared to ask the right questions, organize the right documents, and advocate for your family's future. This preparation translates directly into meaningful, practical outcomes: financial stability, preserved benefit eligibility, and greater peace of mind.

As you continue through this journey, remember that financial planning for a special needs family is not a one-time event. It's a dynamic process that should grow with your child. A coordinated tax strategy—reviewed regularly and guided by professionals—ensures that your financial plan remains resilient, responsive, and tailored to meet your family's unique and changing needs.

Chapter Nine

Planning for Decision

Making and Care Beyond Your Lifetime

The Conversation We Had to Have

There's a certain weight that comes with planning for a future you might not be part of—not because you expect something to happen, but because you know how important it is to be prepared. For a long time, my husband and I pushed that conversation aside. Sometimes out of denial. Most of the time because there was always something more immediate to deal with: therapies, IEP meetings, medical appointments, the daily rhythm of parenting. And yet, the question was always lingering in the background: "*If something happened to us, then what?*"

What finally pushed us to act wasn't a dramatic moment—it was the quiet realization that avoiding these decisions didn't protect anyone. If anything, it created more uncertainty for the people we love. We weren't just planning for our son with special needs—we were planning for his younger brother too. If something ever happened to us, we didn't want our families left guessing. We wanted a plan that considered both of our boys—their care, their relationship, their future. Naming decision-makers, outlining our wishes, and putting the legal pieces in place became the way we could give our family clarity, not just in a crisis, but for the years ahead.

We started with what felt most urgent—naming guardians in our will. Then came conversations with family. Who could realistically take on the role? What support would they need? What would "quality of life" look like through our lens? These weren't easy discussions—but they were grounding. They helped us move from fear to purpose.

As someone who works in this world—financial planning, legacy planning, the "what ifs" of life—I thought I'd be immune to the emotional weight. I wasn't. And that's okay. Because this kind of planning isn't just logistical—it's deeply personal. It asks you to imagine a world where you're no longer present, and to leave behind a roadmap detailed enough to be followed with confidence.

My hope for this chapter is that it helps you begin that process—or refine it if you've already started. Planning for decision-making and care beyond your lifetime isn't something we ever *want* to do, but it's something we *can* do with intention, love, and clarity. Not because we're expecting the worst—but because we're doing our best.

~Ashli
EAVES

Your Child's Road to Adulthood: A New Fork in the Journey

Turning 18 is a milestone for any young person. It represents freedom, responsibility, and the beginning of independence as they legally become adults. For parents of children with special needs, this transition carries extra weight and complexity. In the eyes of the law, your child is now presumed capable of making their own decisions—regardless of their actual cognitive abilities or decision-making capacity.

Think of this legal transition as a switch that flips automatically. On your child's 17th birthday, you still have full legal authority to make medical, financial, and educational decisions for them. The next day—their 18th birthday—that authority vanishes unless you've taken specific legal steps beforehand. This abrupt legal shift can feel like being asked to hand your child the car keys when they've never taken a driving lesson. Suddenly, you're no longer automatically included in medical appointments, school planning meetings, or financial decisions. The safety net you've carefully built starts to disappear—unless you've made specific plans to replace it.

This chapter is about creating that new safety net—one that allows your child to move forward, with you as the guide and planner, even after you're no longer physically present to help navigate the road.

Understanding the legal transition at age 18 is essential because, without appropriate arrangements, you may suddenly lose the ability to help your adult child with special needs make critical life decisions, even if their need for support remains unchanged.

Understanding the Legal Road Map: Common Terms, Simplified

Before we can talk about who might be sitting in the passenger seat, helping your child navigate life's twists and turns, it's helpful to get familiar with the basic legal structures available. To start, here's a snapshot of some common terms:

Guardianship

A guardian is appointed by the court to make decisions for someone who can't do so safely on their own. This includes choices about healthcare, housing, and education.

- Best for: Individuals who cannot manage most aspects of daily life independently.
- Impact on independence: Significant—removes many basic rights.
- Court involvement: Yes, and requires ongoing reporting.

Limited Guardianship

Think of this like partial coverage. The court assigns decision-making only in specific areas—like healthcare or education—while allowing your child to retain control in others.

- Best for: People who need help in only a few areas.
- Impact on independence: Partial; preserves autonomy where possible.

- Court involvement: Yes, but more tailored and flexible.

Conservatorship

Focused specifically on money. A conservator manages financial affairs but doesn't have control over personal decisions.

- Best for: Individuals who handle life well but struggle with managing money.
- Impact on independence: Limited to financial matters.
- Court involvement: Yes, often with regular financial reporting.

Power of Attorney (POA)

A POA is a legal document your child can sign (if they have the mental capacity to do so) that grants someone else the authority to act on their behalf—like managing bank accounts or making healthcare decisions.

- Best for: Individuals who understand their need for help and can make informed decisions.
- Impact on independence: Retains full control unless activated.
- Court involvement: None. It's a private agreement.

Supported Decision-Making (SDM)

This is the least restrictive model. Your child makes their own choices but has a team of trusted people (like a personal advisory board) helping explain options and consequences.

- Best for: Individuals who can make decisions with the right support.

- Impact on independence: Full autonomy.
- Court involvement: Usually not required.

These options aren't one-size-fits-all, and your child may need a different arrangement as they grow and change. What matters most is finding the least restrictive option that still offers enough protection.

Beyond Guardianship: Preserving Autonomy with Alternative Arrangements

Full guardianship isn't the only option for adults with special needs. For many individuals with developmental disabilities, intellectual challenges, or mental health conditions, less restrictive alternatives can provide necessary support while preserving important rights and dignity. These options recognize that capability exists on a spectrum and that many people can make sound decisions with appropriate assistance.

Power of attorney documents offer a flexible alternative for individuals who have the capacity to understand they need help with certain decisions. A durable power of attorney for healthcare allows your adult child to designate you or another trusted person to make medical decisions if they cannot. Similarly, a financial power of attorney grants authority to help manage money matters. These documents can be customized to cover specific areas where support is needed while leaving other decisions in your child's hands.

Supported decision-making represents a newer approach gaining recognition in many states. This model formally acknowledges that people with disabilities can make their own choices when given appropriate information and assistance. Unlike guardianship, which transfers decision-making authority to someone else, supported decision-making keeps the individual at the center of all choices while surrounding them with a team of trusted advisors.

The mechanics of supported decision-making resemble a personal board of directors. Your adult child remains the CEO of their life, but they have advisors for different domains—perhaps you for healthcare decisions, a sibling for housing questions, and a financial professional for money management. These supporters provide information, explain options, and help implement decisions, but the final choice remains with your child. This arrangement is formalized through agreements that can be recognized by medical providers, financial institutions, and service agencies.

Representative payee arrangements offer another targeted solution for individuals who receive government benefits but struggle with financial management. A representative payee, appointed by the Social Security Administration, receives benefit payments on behalf of the beneficiary and uses the funds for essential needs like housing, food, and medical care. This arrangement protects financial resources without removing other rights or decision-making capabilities.

Some families find that simple and practical support is sufficient. Joint bank accounts allow parents to monitor spending and help with bill paying without formal legal arrangements. Automated bill payments, spending cards with limits, and banking alerts can create financial safeguards. For healthcare, HIPAA authorization forms permit doctors to share information with parents or other supporters while still involving the individual in their own care decisions.

Technology increasingly offers promising tools that promote independence with appropriate safeguards. Medication reminder apps, GPS tracking devices, simplified banking applications, and video communication tools allow many individuals with cognitive challenges to live more independently than was possible in previous generations. These technological supports often reduce the need for legal interventions by addressing specific areas of vulnerability.

Finding the right balance between protection and independence represents perhaps the most nuanced challenge in special needs planning. While the instinct to shield your child from all potential harm is natural, excessive restrictions can hamper personal growth and self-determination. The most successful plans provide a flexible framework that can evolve as your child develops new capabilities and as circumstances change. This approach requires honest assessment of your child's abilities, limitations, and potential—often with input from developmental experts who can help identify realistic expectations.

The decisions you make about guardianship and financial oversight will ultimately shape your child's daily life and long-term well-being. When thoughtfully constructed with input from a collaborative team of specialists, these arrangements become more than legal formalities—they transform into a personalized support system that honors your child's unique needs while maximizing their potential for fulfillment. The peace of mind that comes from knowing you've created this protection extends beyond financial security to something far more valuable: the confidence that your child will be understood, respected, and properly supported, even when you're no longer there to advocate for them yourself.

Selecting the Right Co-Pilots: Guardians and Caregivers

When thinking about who could take over decision-making, caregiving, or both, the first question most parents ask is: *"Who could ever know my child the way I do?"*

The truth is—no one will ever replace you. But you can thoughtfully prepare someone to step into the role with confidence, care, and clarity.

Here are a few things to consider:

- Do they know and understand your child already?
- Do they share your values?
- Are they physically and emotionally capable of caregiving?
- Will they advocate for your child?
- Are they likely to be around long-term?

Family members are common choices, but they're not your only option. In some cases, a close family friend, a godparent, or even a professional guardian might be a better fit.

It's also okay to divide responsibilities. One person might be great with financial matters (as a trustee or conservator), while another excels at hands-on caregiving.

Don't forget to have open and honest conversations with potential guardians. Share what's involved, give them time to ask questions, and confirm they're truly willing.

Planning for the Long Road: When You're No Longer Driving

Imagine you're handing someone the keys to a car they've never driven. You wouldn't just walk away—you'd leave behind a manual, point out which buttons to press, and maybe even stay in the passenger seat for a few practice runs. That's exactly what thoughtful planning does for your child's future.

Creating appropriate legal structures is fundamental to ensuring your child's protection after you're gone. These legal mechanisms safeguard benefits eligibility, manage assets, and establish decision-making authority. Understanding your options helps you create a framework that provides both protection and flexibility.

Beyond decision-making, there are additional legal tools that help manage resources and preserve access to vital services. These include:

- Special Needs Trusts (SNTs): These hold assets for your child's benefit without jeopardizing public benefits eligibility. SNTs come in different forms and should be reviewed with an attorney.
- ABLE Accounts: Tax-advantaged savings accounts that allow individuals with disabilities to save for qualified expenses.
- Healthcare Directives: Provide guidance on medical care preferences and ensure continuity in treatment.

- Property and Housing Arrangements: Legal planning around where your child will live, whether it's in your home or a supported setting.
- Letters of Intent: While not legally binding, these documents offer invaluable guidance on your child's routine, needs, and your long-term hopes for them.

The **Letter of Intent**, in particular, acts as your manual for the next caregiver. While it doesn't carry legal authority, it provides detailed personal instructions about how to care for your child. This is your opportunity to share everything you know—from their bedtime routine to how they express discomfort or happiness.

Be sure to include:

- Daily schedules
- Medical needs
- Communication styles
- Triggers and calming strategies
- Preferred foods, activities, or social connections
- Educational and vocational goals
- Your personal hopes and dreams for their future

This document becomes the bridge between your parenting and theirs. It's one of the most meaningful gifts you can leave—not only for your child, but for the people who will love and support them in the future.

A Checklist for Your Journey Planning

Here's a simple action plan to help you begin or continue your decision-making and long-term care planning:

1. **Start Early** – Begin planning before your child turns 18 to avoid lapses in support.

2. **Understand Your Legal Options** – Learn the basics of guardianship, POA, SDM, and more.

3. **Evaluate Your Child's Abilities** – Consider their decision-making skills with input from professionals.

4. **Identify Key Supporters** – Make a list of trusted people who could help now or in the future.

5. **Have the Conversations** – Talk openly with potential guardians or decision-makers about your child's needs.

6. **Work with a Special Needs Attorney** – Get professional guidance for drafting the right documents.

7. **Create Your Letter of Intent** – Document everything a future caregiver would need to know.

8. **Establish a Financial Plan** – Use a trust, insurance, and government benefits to fund care long-term.

9. **Prepare for Transition** – Introduce future caregivers to your child's world gradually.

10. **Review Annually** – Revisit your plan each year and after major life events.

The Destination: A Future with Confidence

Planning for decision-making and long-term care isn't about control—it's about love. It's the road map that ensures your child will have companions on their journey, even if you're not there to lead the way.

As you take these steps, you're not just preparing for what could go wrong. You're investing in a future where your child continues to grow, thrive, and be supported by people who truly understand them.

Remember that this plan isn't static—it will grow and adapt as your child does. The goal isn't perfection but progress toward a future where your child continues to thrive with the support systems you've thoughtfully put in place.

You've already been the driver for so long. Now you're building a system that will keep your child moving forward—even if someone else is behind the wheel.

Chapter Ten

Building a Strong Support Team

I Was Tired of Being the Expert in Everything

For a long time, I thought I had to figure it all out myself. I'm a researcher by nature, a planner at heart. I'd stay up late reading articles, watching webinars, diving into message boards—trying to piece together how to build the perfect plan for our family.

But, somewhere along the way, I hit a wall.

I was the scheduler, the benefits manager, the therapy coordinator, the insurance interpreter, and the educational advocate. I knew the ins and outs of our son's needs better than anyone—but that didn't mean I knew everything about special needs trusts, long-term planning, or how to tie all the legal, medical, and financial pieces together. And honestly, trying to be the expert in everything left me mentally and emotionally drained. You know those t-shirts that say *"Mama Tired"*? That was me.

That's when I realized something important: just because I *could* do a lot on my own didn't mean I *should*.

I started talking to professionals—an attorney who understood special needs law, a care coordinator who had seen what systems look like when they work well. And this is where my own role as a financial professional began to evolve. Yes, part of my desire to dive deeper into this specialized area of planning came from wanting to do better for our own family. But, I also saw a gap—families like ours needed advisors who truly understood this space, and I wanted to be someone who could help fill that gap.

It's funny—I have my own team, but I'm also part of other people's teams. And that's the beauty of this kind of planning. We're not meant to do it alone.

What I've learned is that building a team doesn't mean handing everything over. It means inviting the right people in to walk alongside you—people who ask the questions you didn't know to ask, who catch things you might've missed, and who bring their own expertise so you can focus on being the parent, not the project manager.

You're still the CEO of your child's care—but even CEOs have a team.

~Ashli

You Don't Have to Do This Alone: Why Your Child's Future Depends on Your Team

Parenting a child with special needs can feel like navigating a complex maze without a map. The financial and legal decisions you face are numerous, often technical, and always consequential. This isolation isn't just emotionally taxing—it can lead to costly mistakes and missed opportunities that impact your child's future.

The truth is that no parent, regardless of their background or education, possesses all the specialized knowledge needed to create a comprehensive financial and care plan for a child with special needs. Many parents describe feeling isolated in this planning journey–overwhelmed by information, yet somehow still in the dark. Even personally, as a financial advisor and parent of a child with autism, I still find myself constantly learning, asking questions, and seeking out new information and guidance from colleagues with specific expertise. **Building a strong support team isn't a luxury—it's a necessity for creating a sustainable plan** for your child now and in the future.

In my years working with families, I've observed that parents who attempt to handle everything alone often experience decision paralysis. The fear of making wrong choices becomes so overwhelming that they postpone critical planning steps, sometimes indefinitely. The weight of this responsibility, combined with the day-to-day demands of caregiving, creates an emotional burden that makes clear-headed decision-making difficult.

A well-constructed support team changes this dynamic entirely. With the right professionals guiding you, complex decisions become manageable steps in a structured process. Financial and legal roadmaps transform from abstract concerns into concrete plans with specific actions and timelines. This structured approach doesn't just produce better outcomes—it dramatically reduces the emotional strain of planning, giving you mental space to focus on what matters most: being present for your child today.

Throughout this chapter, we'll explore the essential members of an effective support team. We'll identify how financial advisors, attorneys, care managers, and other professionals can provide the specialized knowledge you need. You'll learn how to evaluate potential team members, including what qualifications to look for and which questions to ask to ensure they truly understand the unique challenges of special needs planning. Most importantly, you'll discover how to coordinate these professionals to work together harmoniously, creating a cohesive strategy rather than disconnected advice.

We'll also address the ongoing nature of this planning process. Your child's needs will evolve, laws will change, and financial circumstances will shift. **A strong support team doesn't just help you create a plan—it helps you maintain and adapt it** as life unfolds. You'll learn practical strategies for keeping your plan updated without overwhelming yourself with constant revisions or meetings.

Building this team requires an investment of time and resources, but the return is immeasurable: peace of mind knowing you've created strategies for a sustainable future for your child, confidence in the decisions you're making today, and relief from carrying the full weight of planning alone. By the end of this chapter, you'll have a clear roadmap for assembling professionals who can translate your deepest hopes for your child into practical, legally sound strategies that will stand the test of time.

Remember: the goal isn't to delegate your responsibility or diminish your role as your child's fiercest advocate. Rather, it's to surround yourself with the expertise that amplifies your advocacy and ensures your efforts create the strongest possible foundation for your child's future. Let's begin plotting the course together.

Creating Your Professional Circle of Trust

Professional advisors form the technical foundation of your child's long-term plan. Think of them as the specialized team that helps you navigate legal, financial, healthcare, educational, and government systems with clarity and purpose. Each expert brings a unique lens to your planning:

- **Financial Advisors**: Especially those trained in special needs planning, help balance government benefit eligibility with private savings, explain the use of ABLE accounts and trusts, and structure long-term strategies for financial security. They help families prioritize financial goals, coordinate with other professionals, and adjust plans as needs change.

- **Attorneys**: Special needs attorneys craft wills, trusts, and guardianship arrangements with the specific language required to protect benefits and define care intentions. They ensure documents comply with current laws and regulations, which frequently change.

- **Care Managers and Healthcare Coordinators**: These professionals help navigate complex healthcare systems, manage insurance claims, and coordinate therapies, acting as medical advocates when needed. Their knowledge of available resources often extends to community support services you might otherwise miss.

- **Educational Consultants**: From securing appropriate school services to planning for transitions, these professionals ensure your child's learning environment supports their development.

- **Government Benefits Specialists**: They guide you through programs like SSI, Medicaid, and vocational rehab, helping you understand eligibility and application strategies.

- **Insurance Professionals**: With experience in special needs planning, they help you evaluate life, disability, and long-term care policies in a way that supports, rather than complicates, your overall plan.

- **Mental Health Professionals**: Therapists and counselors support both your child and your family through the emotional challenges that come with long-term caregiving.

These professionals don't replace your role as a parent or advocate—they amplify your planning efforts and ensure you aren't navigating everything alone.

Finding and Evaluating Expert Guidance

Locating professionals with genuine special needs expertise requires strategic searching beyond generic credentials. Start with referrals from parent support groups, disability organizations, and other families facing similar circumstances. These personal recommendations often lead to professionals who truly understand the unique challenges you face rather than those who merely list *"special needs planning"* as a service offering.

When evaluating potential advisors, look for specific credentials and experience. For financial professionals, designations like Chartered Special Needs Consultant (ChSNC) or Certified Financial Planner (CFP) with demonstrated special needs experience indicate specialized training. Attorneys should have extensive experience in special needs trusts, ABLE accounts, and guardianship matters. Ask how many special needs families they currently serve and request to speak with existing clients if possible.

Choosing the right professional is like choosing the right guide for a mountain climb. You don't want someone who's only read about the trail in guidebooks–you need someone who has walked it, knows the terrain, and can help you navigate the unexpected.

Before committing to work with any professional, schedule initial consultations with several candidates. During these meetings, observe how well they listen and whether they ask thoughtful questions about your unique situation. Do they speak directly to your child when appropriate? Do they show genuine interest in understanding your family's specific circumstances? The right professionals will demonstrate both technical expertise and compassionate understanding.

Be wary of advisors who present cookie-cutter solutions or focus immediately on selling specific products. Qualified special needs planners typically begin with comprehensive information gathering and education before recommending specific strategies. They should freely explain how they're compensated (fees, commissions, or both) and demonstrate transparency about potential conflicts of interest.

When interviewing potential team members, prepare a list of questions that address their experience, approach, and communication style:

- How many families with similar diagnoses or circumstances have you worked with?

- What ongoing education do you pursue to stay current with changing laws and regulations?
- How do you coordinate with other professionals on a client's team?
- What is your communication process, and how frequently will we review the plan?
- How do you address potential conflicts between financial strategies and benefit eligibility?

Consider creating a systematic evaluation framework for potential advisors. Rate each professional on critical factors including expertise, experience, communication style, accessibility, and fee structure. This methodical approach helps cut through emotional decision-making and focuses on finding the best qualified professionals for your needs.

Remember that building your team doesn't happen overnight. Start with the most pressing needs—typically legal and financial guidance—and gradually expand your circle as new requirements emerge. The goal isn't assembling the largest team but creating the right configuration of expertise for your child's specific situation.

Professional chemistry matters tremendously. You'll work closely with these advisors for years, possibly decades, sharing deeply personal information and making difficult decisions together. Choose professionals whose communication style and values align with yours. The best-credentialed advisor might not be the right fit if their approach creates stress or if you don't feel comfortable asking questions.

Geographic proximity isn't necessarily critical. While local professionals offer convenience for in-person meetings and may better understand regional resources, don't sacrifice expertise for location. Many special needs planning specialists work remotely with clients nationwide, using video conferencing and secure document sharing. This expands your options beyond your immediate area.

How would your planning process and peace of mind transform if you surround yourself with professionals who truly understand both the technical aspects and emotional dimensions of special needs planning?

Expanding Your Network Beyond Family

While professionals play a central role, a broader circle of support—community connections, peers, organizations, and neighbors—adds vital layers of protection and presence. This network can provide day-to-day encouragement, emergency backup, and emotional strength for your child and their future caregivers.

- Peer Support Groups: These offer understanding and experience-based insights that complement professional guidance. Successor caregivers can benefit from these networks too.

- Community Organizations: Religious groups, civic clubs, and local nonprofits often provide meaningful support—social connection, volunteer help, and practical assistance during difficult times.

- Disability Service Providers: Relationships with case managers, residential programs, and vocational support staff offer continuity and system-level expertise that families may not have on their own.
- Neighbors and Local Contacts: Even informal relationships can play a powerful role. Some families intentionally cultivate "circles of support" that include local allies who know and care about your child.
- Technology Tools: Smart devices, remote monitoring systems, and virtual check-ins can help expand your child's safety net, especially if family or supporters aren't nearby.
- Educational and Employment Connections: Teachers, job coaches, and employers often have meaningful insight into your child's abilities and needs—insight that can support caregivers during key transitions.

Make It Know and Keep It Current

As you build this network, **document everything**. Keep an up-to-date list of names, roles, contact info, and the type of support each person or organization provides. Share it with trustees, guardians, and caregivers so they know who to reach out to—and how. A well-documented support system offers peace of mind and makes transitions smoother when roles shift or new challenges arise. Remember, this plan is an ongoing process requiring regular review and adjustment. Life circumstances change, laws evolve, and your child's needs shift over time. Without consistent maintenance, even the most carefully crafted plan can become outdated or ineffective.

Most financial professionals recommend reviewing your special needs plan at least annually, with additional check-ins whenever significant life events occur. These events might include changes in your child's health or capabilities, shifts in family circumstances such as divorce or remarriage, adjustments to government benefit programs, changes in household income, or revisions to tax laws affecting special needs planning strategies.

Neglecting to review your plan over time can undermine the very protections you worked so hard to put in place. Outdated legal documents might not reflect current laws, potentially jeopardizing benefit eligibility. Investment strategies that once aligned perfectly with your goals might become inappropriate as your child ages or financial markets shift. Care arrangements that seemed ideal when established might no longer suit your child's developing needs and preferences.

The COMPASS Framework: Coordinated Organization of Multidisciplinary Professionals Actively Supporting Special-Needs Success

To help simplify the process of moving from planning to implementation, let's review the **COMPASS Framework**—a structured, team-based model designed to guide families through special needs planning with clarity, collaboration, and confidence.

Each part of COMPASS reflects a principle that turns theory into action. This framework is designed to be both flexible and durable—like a compass, it doesn't map every twist in the road, but it keeps you heading in the right direction.

C - Core Team Assembly

Build your foundation with trusted professionals experienced in special needs planning—typically including a financial advisor, attorney, care manager, and benefits expert.

O - Organizational Structure

Clarify roles and lines of communication. Assign a lead coordinator (often your advisor or attorney) to keep everyone aligned without taking over individual responsibilities.

M - Multidisciplinary Integration

Ensure your professionals don't work in silos. Encourage collaboration so legal, financial, care, and benefit strategies align seamlessly.

P - Purpose-Driven Planning

Start with a clear vision. Every plan should reflect your family's values and goals—whether that's long-term housing, financial security, or quality of life outcomes.

A - Active Collaboration Protocols

Establish protocols for ongoing communication—joint meetings, shared documents, and regular check-ins. Stay engaged and informed as the leader of your team.

S - Strategic Review Mechanisms

Review your plan regularly. Set a schedule to reassess progress, address changes, and update documents or benefits based on current needs.

S - Success Metrics and Adaptation

Track what matters. Define indicators of progress and adjust your plan as life changes—staying flexible while keeping your long-term goals in focus.

The strength of your special needs planning depends not just on assembling the right professionals but on creating an integrated system where expertise flows seamlessly between team members, adapting continuously to your child's evolving needs while maintaining clear focus on your family's vision for the future.

When to Consider Adjusting Your Support Team

Professional relationships evolve, and, occasionally, you may need to reconsider certain team members. Signs that a change might be necessary include difficulty reaching the professional, recommendations that consistently disregard your priorities, resistance to collaborating with other team members, or failure to stay current with changing regulations affecting special needs planning.

If concerns arise, start with direct communication. Many issues result from misaligned expectations rather than professional inadequacy. Clearly express your needs and concerns, giving the professional opportunity to address them. If problems persist despite these conversations, begin exploring alternatives while ensuring any transition preserves continuity in your planning efforts.

Remember that different life stages may require adjusting your team composition. The professionals who helped establish your initial plan might not be the same ones best suited to guide you through later phases. For example, as your child approaches adulthood, you might add a vocational rehabilitation specialist or housing coordinator to your team, while maintaining relationships with your core financial and legal advisors.

The emotional dimensions of special needs planning deserve as much attention as technical aspects. Your support team should recognize and respect the psychological challenges families face when planning for an uncertain future. Professionals who dismiss these emotional considerations or focus exclusively on technical solutions often miss critical factors affecting implementation and sustainability of recommended strategies.

The professionals guiding your special needs planning must balance technical expertise with genuine understanding of your family's unique circumstances, collaborating seamlessly across disciplines while adapting to changing needs throughout your child's lifetime.

Your Path Forward

Throughout this chapter, we've examined the key professionals who can guide you, practical approaches to finding trustworthy experts, and the critical importance of maintaining your plan through ongoing reviews.

The right team doesn't just provide technical expertise; they offer a steady hand as you navigate important decisions. Financial advisors who understand special needs trusts, attorneys who specialize in disability law, and care coordinators who can navigate complex systems all work together to create a cohesive strategy tailored to your family's unique situation.

Remember that vetting potential advisors requires more than checking credentials. The professionals you select should demonstrate genuine understanding of your child's specific needs and show willingness to collaborate with other team members. Your instincts matter—the right advisors will make you feel heard and respected.

Your financial and legal plan is never truly *"finished."* It's a living, breathing, and evolving plan. Life circumstances change, laws are amended, and your child's needs evolve. Regular reviews—ideally scheduled annually—help ensure your carefully constructed plans remain effective and relevant. These check-ins aren't about starting over but rather fine-tuning what you've built.

When your team is working well, you'll notice a profound shift. The weight of uncertainty begins to lift. Decisions become clearer. You'll find yourself thinking not just about immediate concerns but confidently planning for your child's long-term future.

This roadmap you're creating does more than organize finances and legal documents—it provides a foundation for your child's wellbeing that extends beyond your direct care. By assembling and maintaining the right support team, you're creating a structure that will stand firm even when you cannot be there yourself.

The time and effort invested now in building these professional relationships yields invaluable dividends: **reduced stress, increased confidence, and the profound reassurance that comes from knowing**

you've taken concrete steps to secure your child's future. Your advocacy today creates protection for tomorrow.

Take the next steps outlined in this chapter. Reach out to potential advisors, schedule those initial consultations, and begin assembling the team that will help chart your course forward. Your child deserves nothing less than thoughtful, expert guidance—and so do you.

Chapter Eleven

From Planning to Practice

From Scattered to Steady

I've always been a planner. I had notes in my phone, spreadsheets on my laptop, a folder for every piece of paperwork, and plenty of color-coded checklists. It wasn't that things were chaotic—it was that everything existed in its own lane. Remember how, at the beginning of this book, I shared how my personal and professional life once felt like two separate paths? That's exactly how I used to think about all the topics we've covered here—legal, financial, educational, emotional. I had touched each piece at some point, but I hadn't yet stepped back to see how they were meant to fit together.

But slowly—piece by piece—things started to come together. Not all at once, and definitely not perfectly. I'd research special needs trusts one week, dig into tax strategies the next, then circle back to life insurance. It felt like I was making progress, but it wasn't always clear how one part connected to the next. The picture was forming, but it still felt like a collection of puzzle pieces I hadn't fully assembled.

Eventually, I started to see things come into focus. We created a will. We named guardians. We opened an ABLE account. We chose life insurance policies with intention. We began thinking about how our children—both of our children—would be cared for in the future. Because this plan was never just about our son with special needs. It was about both of our sons. One may need more structure and support, but both deserve thoughtful planning, protection, and possibility.

And for the first time, it felt like we weren't just making decisions in isolation. We were building something comprehensive—something aligned.

It still evolves. Plans shift as family shifts. But having something in place—a foundation—brings a peace that's hard to explain. It's not that all the worry disappears. It's that you finally feel like you've taken the wheel, even on a road that still has curves ahead.

This chapter isn't about having everything figured out. It's about creating a framework, understanding the moving parts, and giving yourself credit for every single step you've already taken. Because when it comes to any kind of financial planning, progress is the goal—not perfection.

~Ashli
EAVES

Navigating from Knowledge to Action

By now, you've journeyed through the complexities of special needs financial planning—from understanding benefit eligibility to structuring trusts, building your team, and organizing for the long term. This final chapter isn't about revisiting every detail. Instead, it's your guide for turning insight into action.

The most meaningful plans don't just sit in a binder or a shared folder—they come to life through consistent steps and shared intention. When those steps are guided by your family's values and implemented by a team that understands your unique situation, planning becomes less about compliance and more about creating clarity and confidence for the road ahead.

Common Roadblocks (And How to Overcome Them)

Even with the best intentions, it's easy to fall into **procrastination** or **paralysis by analysis**. Here are a few common roadblocks and how to push past them:

"I don't have time for this right now."
You don't have to do everything at once. **Start with one small step**—schedule a meeting, research trusts, or open an ABLE account.

"I'm afraid of making the wrong decision."
The worst decision is no decision at all. **Take action, and adjust as needed.** Nothing is set in stone.

"It feels too overwhelming."
Go back to the chapters that apply to your immediate situation. Focus on just **one task at a time.**

Remember, **progress is more important than perfection.**

Acknowledging the Challenges

I would be remiss not to acknowledge that even with this financial roadmap, the path ahead contains uncertainties. Government programs change. Tax laws evolve. Medical advances may alter your child's prognosis and needs. The professional team you've carefully assembled may experience turnover.

These variables aren't reasons to abandon planning—they're reminders of why flexible, resilient planning is so vital. The framework you've built can absorb these changes because it's founded on principles rather than rigid prescriptions.

There will also be moments when the emotional weight of planning for a future you won't fully share with your child feels overwhelming. During these times, remember that your advance planning is perhaps the most profound expression of your love and commitment.

Building Your Implementation Timeline

Many families find that three to six months is a realistic and manageable timeframe to put a strong plan in place. Here's a general outline to help pace your progress:

Month 1: Clarify & Connect

- Organize financial and legal documents
- Meet with your spouse or family to define shared goals
- Begin interviewing professionals for your planning team

Months 2–3: Legal & Foundational Work

- Draft or update key documents: Special Needs Trust, wills, powers of attorney

- Create your letter of intent
- Confirm guardianship arrangements and beneficiary designations

Months 4–5: Strategy & Funding

- Work with your advisor to estimate long-term needs and investment targets
- Adjust insurance coverage for income protection and trust funding
- Set up funding pathways: ABLE accounts, life insurance, savings plans

Month 6: Communication & Integration

- Create a simple plan summary to share with trusted family members
- Hold a family meeting (when appropriate) to explain how others can support your plan
- Schedule ongoing review sessions with your advisor and legal team

This phased approach helps you build momentum without feeling overwhelmed. If you've already completed some of these steps, that's great—use this as a tool to identify what comes next.

Keeping Your Plan Aligned

In earlier chapters, we highlighted *"critical mistakes"* to avoid. But let's reframe that. Planning is rarely perfect, especially in complex, emotionally charged areas like this. What matters more is being **proactive** rather than reactive. Here are a few reminders as you move forward:

- **Keep accounts in your name or your trust's name, not your child's.** This helps protect benefits.
- **Review your beneficiary designations.** Make sure they align with your overall strategy.
- **Choose fiduciaries thoughtfully.** Pick trustees and guardians who understand your values and responsibilities.
- **Communicate your plan.** Silence can lead to unintended disruptions—share only what's appropriate, but don't assume people know your wishes.
- **Start, even if it's small.** Progress beats perfection every time. A basic, flexible plan is far better than none at all.

These reminders aren't warnings—they're guideposts. Every step you take helps strengthen the financial and emotional stability of your child's future.

Looking Ahead With Confidence

You've made it to the end of this book—but, more importantly, you've committed to taking steps that many never do. You've chosen to lead with love and plan with purpose. That choice is powerful.

The greatest gift you can give your child isn't a perfect plan—it's a thoughtful one: one that reflects your values, secures their needs, and prepares others to step in when you can't. That kind of planning creates more than financial protection. It creates legacy.

As you begin this planning journey, know that confidence comes not from having all the answers, but from knowing you've taken the time to ask the right questions—and surrounded yourself with people who can help you answer them. That's not just smart planning. That's exceptional parenting.

Epilogue

If you've made it this far, I want to pause and say thank you—not just for reading, but for showing up. For your child. For your family. And for yourself.

I didn't write this book from the perspective of a detached professional. I wrote it as someone who's walked this road, too. I know what it feels like to be overwhelmed by acronyms and options. To lie awake wondering if I'm providing the best I can for our family. To wrestle with decisions that feel both deeply personal and entirely unfamiliar.

What I've learned—and what I hope this book has shown—is that you don't have to do it all at once. Planning for your child's future doesn't require perfection, but it does require love, consistency, and a willingness to take the next step.

You've reached the end of our journey together—through the valleys and peaks of special needs planning. What may have begun as a confusing trek filled with legal requirements, financial questions, and care coordination has now become a clearer roadmap for your family's future.

Your Greatest Legacy

As we close this book, I want to pause and recognize the significance of what you've accomplished.

Financial planning for a child with special needs is not just a technical or financial exercise. It's an extension of your love. It's your way of continuing to show up—even in a future you may not get to see.

You've had hard conversations. You've made decisions many would rather postpone. You've built something enduring: a plan that reflects your values, protects your child, and equips others to carry on your care.

This isn't just a plan. It's a legacy.

Take a moment to acknowledge what you've accomplished. You've earned it. The peace of mind that comes with preparation isn't just for your child—it's for you, too. We may not have landed where we thought we would, but we've learned to appreciate the charm of this place—the pace, the people, the purpose. Holland has its own rhythm, and over time, it becomes home. The journey may look different, but it's still rich and full of love. I'm honored to share the view from Holland with you.

***"A mother's love for her child is like nothing else in the world. It knows no law, no pity. It dares all things and crushes down remorselessly all that stands in its path."* - Agatha Christie**

Chapter Twelve

What you should do now...

Here's How To Navigate Finances, Legalities, and Care for Your Special Child Without Feeling Overwhelmed.

WE'VE REACHED THE END of our time together, my friend. I hope this book has brought you clarity, encouragement, and a renewed sense of direction.

The next step for you is simple:

Get started!

Taking that first step is the most important part of the journey. Planning doesn't need to be perfect—it just needs to begin. With the knowledge and tools you've gained, you're now better equipped to protect, plan, and provide for your child's future with greater clarity and purpose.

If you're feeling unsure about where to start—or if you're ready to take the next step but want guidance—know that you don't have to do this alone. I help families at all stages of the journey build thoughtful, personalized financial strategies that support both immediate needs and long-term goals. Whether you're just beginning to explore planning options or looking to strengthen what you've already put in place, I'd be honored to be part of your team.

This process can feel overwhelming, but support is available. If there's something in this book you'd like to better understand—or if you're wondering how it applies to your own situation—I invite you to reach out. I offer a free Initial Chat where we can talk through where you are now and what steps might come next. You can reach me at ashli@alignedwg.com. While I don't provide legal or tax advice, I regularly collaborate with attorneys, care professionals, and other specialists, and I'm happy to help connect you with the right people.

Whether you're just beginning or revisiting your plan with fresh eyes, here's how we can move forward—one thoughtful step at a time:

Step 1: We identify your financial goals and priorities as a caregiver and family.

Step 2: Together, we design an investment strategy tailored to your needs and objectives.

Step 3: We make sure that strategy fits into your busy life—realistic, flexible, and effective.

Step 4: We continue to monitor and adjust your plan so it stays aligned with your family's journey.

With the right plan and the right support, you can live an empowered, joyful life while preparing confidently for what lies ahead.

Let's talk about what a thoughtful financial strategy could look like for your family. You can schedule your Initial Chat by emailing me at ashli@alignedwg.com.

About the Author

Who is Ashli Eaves...

Ashli Eaves – Partnering with Families for Tailored Special Needs Planning

For families raising a child with special needs, financial planning isn't just about numbers—it's about preparing for a future rooted in dignity, care, and thoughtful intention. As a parent of a special needs child and former educator, Ashli Eaves understands this at the deepest level. With both professional expertise and personal experience, she has made it her mission to help families navigate the complex financial landscape of special needs planning with clarity, confidence, and a customized approach that honors their unique journey.

As a dedicated Financial Advisor in Mid-Missouri and a Chartered Special Needs Consultant (ChSNC), Ashli specializes in working with high-earning families who are deeply invested in doing what's best for their children but often feel overwhelmed by the complexity of planning for the future. Many of her clients earn incomes which disqualify them from government assistance programs, leaving them to shoulder the financial burden of care, education, and long-term planning on their own. They know they need a solid plan, but where to start, who to trust, and how to make the right decisions feels daunting.

Special Needs Planning *Is* Financial Planning

While Ashli's work centers on supporting families with special needs, the planning process goes far beyond a single focus. A well-designed special needs plan is, at its core, a holistic financial plan—one that integrates every aspect of a family's goals, values, and responsibilities. From retirement planning and college savings to investment strategies and estate design, Ashli helps families bring all the pieces together into one coordinated approach. Because when you're raising a child with unique needs, every financial decision touches the entire family—and a thoughtful, integrated plan can create stability and confidence for everyone.

Her process provides a clear, step-by-step framework that helps parents:

- Build a financial strategy that helps prepare for their child's future without sacrificing the rest of the family's financial well-being
- Create a plan that supports their child into adulthood—whether that means independence, supported living, or lifelong care
- Navigate special needs trusts, guardianship considerations, and estate planning to ensure protection when they're no longer here
- Understand how to balance financial responsibilities—from saving for other children's college to planning for their own

retirement

- Feel supported and informed as they make thoughtful decisions for their child and their entire family.

A Trusted Partner in an Overwhelming Journey

Many families feel lost when it comes to assembling the right team of professionals to help them—lawyers, financial planners, therapists, and advocates. Ashli serves as a central guide, helping families understand who they need on their team and ensuring that every piece of the puzzle—financial, legal, and personal—is aligned.

She also understands the emotional burden that comes with this journey. The guilt, the exhaustion, the weight of making every decision count. That's why she doesn't just offer financial advice—she offers reassurance, empowerment, and a plan that families can truly feel good about.

Why Families Choose Ashli

Her clients don't just choose her for her financial expertise; they choose her because she gets it. She understands the fears that keep parents up at night:

- *"What happens when I'm no longer here?"*
- *"How can I make sure my child is protected, cared for, and financially secure?"*
- *"Am I doing enough?"*

With Ashli, families gain more than a financial advisor—they gain a trusted ally who is deeply committed to helping them build a secure future. She takes a compassionate, no-judgment approach, ensuring that families feel heard, supported, and empowered at every stage of the planning process.

Helping You Take the First Step Toward Confidence

Many parents put off financial planning because it feels too overwhelming. Ashli makes the process approachable, actionable, and clear. With her guidance, families go from feeling lost and uncertain to having a plan they can rely on—one that protects their child for life.

Whether you're just starting your financial journey or need a strategic plan to secure your child's long-term future, Ashli Eaves is here to guide you every step of the way.

Your child's future deserves a plan. Let's create it together.

Schedule an Initial Chat and take the first step toward building a thoughtful plan rooted in your family's goals and values.

Ashli and her husband, Sean, live in Columbia, Missouri with their two boys and their Goldador (a mellow mix of Golden Retriever and Black Lab). These days, life moves at the pace of carpools and community events, with moments of joy found in Mizzou game days, lakeside escapes (from the Ozarks to Lake Michigan), hot yoga sessions, page-turning books, and the and the ongoing hunt for the next great local brewery.

Ashli is a registered representative of and offers securities through Cambridge Investment Research, Inc., a broker/dealer, member

FINRA/SIPC and advisory services through Cambridge Investment Research Advisors, Inc., a Registered Investment Advisor.

Made in the USA
Monee, IL
09 June 2025

19116140R00100